Words in edgeways

Radical learning for social change

Words in edgeways

Radical learning for social change

Jane Thompson

With a Foreword by Helena Kennedy QC

NIACE
THE NATIONAL ORGANISATION
FOR ADULT LEARNING

Published by the National Institute of Adult Continuing Education
(England and Wales)
21 De Montfort Street, Leicester, LE1 7GE
Company registration no. 2603322
Charity registration no. 1002775

First published 1997

CATALOGUING IN PUBLICATION DATA
A CIP record for this title is available from the British Library
ISBN 1 86201 013 7

Typeset by The Midlands Book Typesetters
Text design by Virman Man
Cover design by Sue Storey
Printed in Great Britain by Antony Rowe Ltd, Chippenham, Wilts

Foreword

In Margaret Atwood's novel, *The Handmaid's Tale*, she creates a futuristic world with intense social divisions. In this chilling vision, she describes those who are powerless as those 'who lived in the blank white spaces on the edge of the print'. It is a haunting image of people at the margin, in the periphery, people who are never part of the story.

Jane Thompson brings those people into the narrative and is a powerful advocate for the role of education in including those who have no voice. Her writing which is vivid and accessible challenges us to see that the current obsession with measuring and auditing achievement works as an inhibitor of the very learning which changes lives.

Those of us who were the first in our families to stay on at school and enter higher education need no persuading of the transformative power of education. The opportunity for further learning not only changed our chances economically but gave us a sense of ourselves, a tolerance of difference and an appreciation of what made the world tick.

The Scottish education system in which I was schooled always recognised that one of the purposes of education was the development of the 'democratic intellect'. Learning was not only to improve one's job prospects but to acquire other skills for life and one of those was the ability to question critically the world around us and its institutions.

In a society where unregulated markets rule and social divisions are growing daily, talk of community fragmentation is rife but little is done to recreate social cohesion. More and more people feel disengaged, ignored in the political discourse. The economic arguments for education take primacy over those which present education as the means of strengthening civil society and securing positive political change. Little cogniscance is given to the growing recognition internationally that social capital is essential to economic success. Jane Thompson eloquently argues for the kind of education which makes for political awareness and social connection.

Through my own experiences in the criminal courts and my recent work looking at how to achieve wider participation in further education, it has become clear to me that maximising the potential of as many people as possible throughout their adult life, as well as being an issue of social justice, is the key to social well-being. However, we have sadly been neglecting the adult education sector where this work of inclusive learning goes on. The second chances offered by further education to the unemployed, to women, to disenfranchised youth, to ethnic minorities and the working class is constantly squeezed because there are other priorities.

In '*Words in Edgeways*', Jane Thompson draws together a collection of her writings which are both provocative and inspirational. She challenges many of the prevailing attitudes which underpin education policy and impeaches the reforms which she sees running counter to 'real' education. These are words which may come in edgeways but will infiltrate the final text.

Helena Kennedy QC

A word in edgeways . . .

In hard times for adult education during the 1980s and 1990s, there has been a range of possible reactions. One has been opportunistic: shifting learners from one place to another, say from community education into an FE College, or from a general syllabus into a national vocational qualification, and calling that growth. Another has been defensive. We are precious, some professionals have said. Potential students, let alone paymasters, may not be able to see how great we are, so we will bury our heads in the sand, until better times come. Another has been bewilderment, leading to draining of energy because it is all too difficult in complicated post-modern times.

So much for at least two centuries of a tradition which goes back through Nonconformity to before the Reformation, and which has produced sharp, energetic critiques of dominant knowledges as well as branches, institutes, societies, events, workshops, meetings and all those creative cells through which any decent society carries its own successor, struggling to get out.

Jane Thompson knows about this history, locates herself within it, has a confident – dare I say beguiling? – manner about her which overcomes despair and gets new things done. Hers has been a magnificent presence at Ruskin since 1993, helping to shift the culture of the college without the slightest hint of selling out. Jane's is a contagious practical, applied consciousness. She was the first person I met who knew what I meant when I put the phrase 'really useful knowledge' into Ruskin's strategic plan and who used the same kind of language. For Jane, it was, and is, much more real and immediate. And more radically gendered. She, like the sisters and brothers from that earlier movement who invented the term 'social science' as a socialist critique of anti-social science, is still into the proposition that things (unequal social relations), can be changed. And tomorrow, not in the next century. I would understand if Jane took another period in her life away from adult education writing novels as she does, innovating in another bit of the world away from Ruskin, but I hope she doesn't. Read on . . .

Stephen Yeo
Principal
Ruskin College, Oxford

Contents

Adult education and the disadvantaged

Originally published in *Adult Education for a Change*,
ed Jane Thompson, Hutchinson, 1980

In 1980 **Adult Education for a Change** brought together leading left wing and radical critics of current thinking in Adult Education, including Keith Jackson, Nell Keddie, Sallie Westwood, Martin Yarnit and Tom Lovett. The book helped to endorse radical practice in a difficult political decade and is referenced in countless student dissertations and sister publications. Its main contribution was to encourage the application of Marxist, sociological and feminist analysis to adult education provision at a time when the dominant definitions of reality and practice relied on liberal perspectives, human growth and behaviourist theories of adult learning.

Thompson's chapter on 'Adult Education and the Disadvantaged' challenges many of the prevailing assumptions upon which provision, post-Russell and in the early phase of the National Literacy Campaign, was based. She identifies the prevailing tendency to pathologise and generalise the 'personality traits' said to be associated with disadvantage in ways which seek to hold the poor responsible for their own inadequacies. In more liberal times, social intervention by professionals with basic skills and community development in mind – albeit on an extremely low cost and piecemeal basis – was a well known response, and was intended to provide various kinds of 'compensatory education' and to restore 'personhood'. Thompson is highly critical of both the analysis and the practice flowing from it – which takes no account of either the structural or material concomitants of inequality.

Whilst the examples she uses are drawn from the context of the late seventies her analysis still has considerable redolence in contemporary, now more punitive, intent to stigmatise and isolate minority groups within the so-called 'underclass' and at a time when the academic fashion for post modernism also fails to draw much attention to continuing structural and material determinants of disadvantage.

Adult education and the disadvantaged

The rediscovery of poverty and the concept of deprivation

The poor, it is said, are always with us, but it is only recently that they have become fashionable. In the wake of Macmillan's 'you've-never had-it-so-good' Britain and the liberal polemicism of Kennedy's campaigning America, Britain in the 1960s 'rediscovered' poverty.

The first soundings of alarm came from a number of commissions of inquiry set up by the government to consider London's housing (Milner and Holland), children and young people (Ingleby), primary education (Plowden), the personal social services (Seebohm), and people and planning (Skeffington). One after the other the reports told the same sad story of bad housing, urban decay, educational disaster areas, unacceptable levels of poverty – in a phrase 'urban deprivation'.

The discovery of the problem of urban deprivation led in rapid succession to a vocabulary of complementary diseases – 'areas of special need', 'pockets of deprivation', 'twilight zones', 'priority areas', etc. Their inhabitants were variously referred to as 'the disadvantaged', 'the under-privileged', the 'culturally', 'environmentally', 'linguistically' and 'educationally deprived', 'the needy', 'the maladjusted' and 'the handicapped'. As Rutter and Madge point out, deprivation became one of the most overworked words in the English language.[1] Bowlby had used it earlier to refer to lack of mother love.[2] Casler saw it as a lack of sensory stimulation.[3] Runciman discussed deprivation in terms of financial and material resources.[4] And Eckland and Kent defined it in terms of deviation from what is considered to be normal and appropriate by dominant groups in society.[5] In the same vein Ginsberg and others discounted the whole notion of deprivation as a myth based on middle-class misconceptions about poor people.[6]

One of the effects of the over-use of words like deprivation and disadvantage has been the tendency to use them as a form of shorthand, lumping together a wide range of precariously related and generally denigratory tendencies into a common stereotype. Maternal deprivation, for example, 'has been used to cover almost every kind of undesirable interaction between mother and child rejection, hostility, cruelty, over-indulgence, repressive control, lack of affection and the like.'[7] In fact, 'the words almost function as a pejorative test in which each reads into the concept his own biases and prejudices.'[8] All of this could well be dismissed as 'academic semantics' were it not for the fact that behind the labels, the oversimplification and the stigma are people who, for whatever reason, continue to experience various forms of personal and social hardship.

In 1972, Sir Keith Joseph, then Secretary of State for Social Services, voiced what, in the circumstances, was considered to be a logical appraisal of the deprivation/disadvantage debate. He asked, 'Why is it, in spite of long periods of full employment and relative prosperity and the improvement of community services since the Second World War, deprivation and problems of maladjustment so conspicuously persist?' He was referring by deprivation to those circumstances which prevent people developing to nearer their potential – physically, emotionally and intellectually' and which reveal themselves in 'poverty, in emotional impoverishment, in personality disorder, in poor educational attainment, in depression and despair'. His conclusion was simple – in the majority of cases, the symptoms of the disease deprivation were endemic in the poor and transmitted from one generation to the next in a 'cycle of deprivation' exacerbated by the feckless, apathetic and disorganised behaviour of those involved. He has of course gone on to clarify his association of deprivation with a form of personal pathology, transmitted from one generation to the next, and to recommend that every effort should be made to prevent those concerned from reproducing themselves in such irresponsibly large numbers. Needless to say the logic and persuasion of Sir Keith Joseph's view of a 'cycle of transmitted deprivation' has come under strong fire, not only because of its racist undertones, but because it seems to link poverty with maladjustment. Nonetheless, the insinuation that poverty and deprivation are a direct consequence of personally derived inadequacy still underpins a good deal of the continuing debate about deprivation and disadvantage.

An additional consequence has been the extent to which the government has felt compelled to intervene and be seen to be responding positively to the recommendations made by commissions, academics and social planners. The introduction of Urban Aid, the setting up of the National Community Development Project and the identification of five Educational Priority Areas were the most famous of a number of projects designed to

> provide for the care of our citizens who live in the poorest parts of our cities and towns . . . to arrest, in so far as it is possible by financial means, and reverse the downward spiral which afflicts so many of these areas (and in which) there is a deadly quagmire of need and apathy.[9]

The CDP was described as

> a neighbourhood-based experiment aimed at finding new ways of meeting the needs of people living in areas of high social deprivation . . . by bringing together the work of the social services underthe leadership of a special project team and also by tapping resources of self-help and mutual help which may exist among the people in the neighbourhoods.[10]

About the same time as the Urban Aid Programme was being set up, the DES announced that an action research project based on five areas of educational priority was to be undertaken. The scheme was part of the national programme of EPAs promoted by the Plowden Report. The DES decided on five special project areas identified in terms of their proportion of low income, low-status families, poor amenities in the home, high demand for free school meals and large numbers of children with language problems. The purpose of the projects was to offer 'positive discrimination' in an attempt to compensate for the inadequacy of the children's home background and in an attempt to make them more susceptible to the benefits of education.

In all of these initiatives there were related and important assumptions motivating the interventions. The final report of the Coventry CDP identified them as:

1   *Disadvantaged areas are a minor blot on the urban landscape.*
2   *The problem can be blamed partly on the apathy or abnormality of local residents and partly on the incompetence of local government.*
3   *The solutions lie in self-help and more active participation by local people and more sensitive services and better communication and coordination on the part of the local authority.*
4   *Solutions can be found at very little extra cost and that a carrot and stick approach by central government can spur the local authorities to do things better in the future.*[11]

All of the initiatives were littered with the language of 'protect' and 'experiment', emphasising the essentially temporary and tokenistic nature of their provision. And despite a good deal of public relations propaganda about 'positive discrimination' they operated on an incredibly small budget. The whole Urban Aid Programme (of which the CDP formed only a small part) represented only one twentieth of one per cent of total public spending, and only one tenth of one per cent of total social service spending. Moreover the Urban Aid Programme was not additional money. It was deducted from the total rate support grant generally available for local authority spending. The EPA project lasted three years between 1968 and 1971 and cost the DES and the SSRC a mere £175,000.

The co-ordination of local authority services was seen as another important feature of strategies designed to relieve poverty and disadvantage. Seebohm had promoted the idea of a generic approach to provision in the personal social services. Better cooperation at local level between those of the various 'caring professions' and local authorities was seen as a good way of streamlining provision and concentrating resources. 'Participation' was another key word, designed to challenge the latent apathy of the poor and galvanise them into constructive self-help activities.

It's hardly surprising that in this climate of opinion, the conscience of adult education was stirred into action, and the relevance of existing adult education provision was called into question.

Adult education and the disadvantaged

In 1973 the Russell Committee published its Plan for Development in adult education. The fact that this report represented only one of four major collections of
information, reviews of provision and recommendations about policy in adult education this century, has made it of critical importance to all those involved in adult
education.[12] During the preceding twenty years or so adult education seemed to many
of those engaged in it to have lost some of its earlier momentum.[13] Although the
1944 Education Act had been quite specific about the duties of local education
authorities with regard to primary, secondary and further education, it didn't actually
mention adult education by name. All of this contributed to the sense of insecurity
and insignificance which many people felt about adult education and why the policy
statements made by Russell were seized upon with such eagerness and gratitude.

As part of the preparation for its general report, the Russell Committee called
for an inquiry to be carried out by Peter Clyne, directed by Henry Arthur Jones,
based at the University of Leicester, and funded by the DES, to provide information
about 'the education of the handicapped, and especially the informal educative influences upon him.'[14] Those involved began with the assumption that access to adult
education was generally and widely available to the 'normal' population although its
quality and quantity might vary in different places.

> *The test of disadvantage then was to identify factors **in the individual or in
> his personal circumstances** that would prevent him from participating in
> whatever the quality of the local provision of classes. The factors lie in three
> main areas: physical and mental handicap, which may be temporary or
> permanent; social disadvantage, which would include geographical isolation
> as well as poverty of life in areas of multiple deprivation; and educational
> disadvantage, which would include illiteracy, linguistic problems such as those
> of immigrants or the born deaf, or **a residual hostility to the whole idea
> of education.** [my emphasis]*[15]

As in all the other circumstances discussed above, the notion of disadvantage was
uncritically related to a wide range of physical and personal defects and social conditions in which diverse groups were linked together, and by which complex social,
economic and political manifestations of inequality went unchallenged. The
consequence was to reduce them all into a single uncomplicated category – 'the
disadvantaged'.

The language of 'personal deficit', 'affliction' and the need for 'treatment' to
'rehabilitate' the 'malfunctioning' adult into 'normal' society runs like a medical
checklist through the literature. The tone is one of mission and concern for the less
fortunate, in areas in which the 'distinctions between therapeutic, educational and
welfare needs become very difficult to establish'.[16]

The results of Clyne's inquiries became central to the recommendations of the
Russell Report. The thinking behind them is more elaborately revealed in his book,
The Disadvantaged Adult. The thrust of his argument is to present the view that adult
education 'is a community service which can effectively bridge the gap between
education and the social services'. Adult education is about aiding 'the individual

towards self-fulfilment, self-confidence and a more capable involvement in [his] family and community'. 'Adult education must be concerned with people as human beings and not primarily as drivers, shop assistants, office workers or executives.' It must provide a 'tool to enable individuals to live their lives in a more informed and contented way as members of the community'.

'But on the fringes of adult education are the millions of men and women who, because of physical or mental disability or social or cultural disadvantage, do not, and cannot, participate in the general programme of adult education.' 'Many of [their] problems can be traced back to, and explained by, the home or the neighbourhood environment.' These are the 'Newsom adults', the 'unclubbables' and the 'drop outs' 'who have failed to understand, maintain contact with, or become involved in, the rapidly changing technological society'. In such circumstances 'there is ample evidence of a cumulative deficit – the passing on from one generation to the next the disadvantages of poverty, unemployment, poor schools, etc', of problems of 'inadequate vocabulary and the inability to articulate', and the 'many symptoms of individual, family and community malfunctioning'.

In such circumstances, Clyne concludes that 'disadvantage and degradation will increase if left unattended'. The intervention of adult education in close co-operation with the social services and community workers is the solution. Adult education can and must provide 'a compensatory and remedial education service' designed to help the disadvantaged 'improve their physical and mental welfare' so that they can achieve 'personal fulfilment, social usefulness and contentment as members of a community [with] the ability to contribute to, rather than take from, the national wealth'.[17]

The Russell Report's attention to the educational needs of the disadvantaged is clearly a testimony to the influence of Henry Arthur Jones and Peter Clyne. The committee's recommendations to the WEA that it should become increasingly responsible for work with the disadvantaged, and to the service generally, that it should attempt to co-operate much more closely with the social services and voluntary agencies, have become important guidelines.[18] The impetus given to creating posts of special responsibility for 'organising the disadvantaged' and the recognition that 'community education' had a part to play, has encouraged – if it needed any more encouragement – yet more support for the 'community solution' to problems of structural poverty.

The outcomes of the committee's recommendations have been two-fold. The reaction of those persuaded by their logic has been to proliferate a whole range of new initiatives, everything from the National Literacy Campaign and its more recent offspring Basic Education[19] to a multitude of small-scale, localised projects designed to meet the challenge of 'Russell category work'.

The other outcome has been to see the recommendations almost totally ignored, not because of their dubious custodialism, but by the dead weight of institutional complacency, fearful of such developments in case they divert limited educational resources towards community education and other innovatory projects and 'away from the more traditional role' of adult education when 'it is by no means established that community education is a desirable or viable replacement'.[20] Wiltshire and Mee are fearful that traditional provision, attracting as it does lower-middle and middle class students on the one hand, and offset by a shift of resources towards the disadvantaged on the other hand, will neglect the vast majority of the population in the middle which adult education ought to be serving.[21] It's astonishing how in this respect – as with the CDPs and the EPAs referred to earlier – exaggerated claims about positive discrimination have led many to believe that vast sums of money are being squandered on the essentially feckless and have confirmed 'the bottomless pit' hypothesis.[22] But in fact, as A. H. Halsey has frequently pointed out, considering the enormity of the problems encountered the magnitude of the aims outlined and the height of the expectations raised, the amounts of money actually forthcoming have been minuscule.

Much more significant than either of these reactions to Russell has been the general acceptance of the assumptions upon which the committee based its assessment of disadvantage. This generally uncritical view of pathological and personalised explanations of disadvantage has served, as it did in explanations of the failure of working-class children in the school system, and the half-hearted response of successive governments to urban deprivation, to divert attention away from a more fundamental examination of the structural causes of poverty, inequality and educational divisiveness in our society.

However unsatisfactory it might appear to be, the notion of disadvantage has many strengths when it comes to educational and governmental intervention. Because it's a term used to refer to a 'multitude of sins', so far as policy makers are concerned, it has the capacity to appeal to a wide range of people with varied and conflicting ideologies. To social and political liberals it indicates the need for initiatives based on optimistic progressivism and couched in terms of 'compensatory education' and 'positive discrimination' in favour of 'deprived groups'. Even to political and social conservatives, educational provision for the disadvantaged has the attraction of being cheap and conciliatory and intended to transform the feckless and potentially disruptive into more responsible citizens. Such expectations are of course not new. Education has frequently been seen as the popular solution to social and political ills.[23] Christopher Jencks commenting on the American 'war on poverty' during the Kennedy/Johnson era – a campaign that did much to influence the thinking and practice in Britain – has suggested that its intention was essentially conservative in that it aimed to educate the poor to change their 'wrong skills, places of residence, personality traits and fertility patterns and to provide "character building" in lower-middle class virtues'.[24] So far as middle-class America was concerned the belief was that if 'they' were just more like 'us' everything would be all right.[25]

In recent years this view of cultural deprivation and disadvantage has come under fierce attack in both America and Britain. Friedman in America[26] and Bernstein in Britain[27] have both argued that cultural deprivation is an inaccurate term, in that no one can be deprived of a culture which every individual possesses, however different it may be from mainstream culture.[28] Kenneth Clark has argued that the labelling of people as deprived and disadvantaged is used as a kind of alibi to cover up the deficiencies of the education system.[29] Bernstein makes the same point when he says 'how can we talk of offering compensatory education to [people] who in the first place have not, as yet, been offered an adequate educational environment?' The concept of compensatory education 'serves to direct attention away from the internal organisation of the educational [system] and focuses attention on families . . . [who] are regarded as deficit systems.'[30]

William Ryan suggests that the ideology of deprivation and disadvantage 'makes it seem that unemployment, poverty, poor education and slum conditions *result* from family breakdown, cultural deprivation and a lack of acculturation'.[31] To sustain the ideology, it is necessary to engage in the popular sport of 'savage discovery', and to fit the theory savages are being discovered all over the place. 'The all-time favourite savage in America is the promiscuous mother who produces a litter of illegitimate brats' in order to benefit from welfare subsidies. The British equivalent would no doubt be the 'isolated' and 'apathetic' residents of vast council estates, prisoners' wives, ethnic minorities and single parents, all identified by their 'obvious inadequacy' and beloved by those engaged in basic education and Russell category work.

In many respects the definitions of disadvantage used by adult educators reflect the worst aspects of individualistic and pathological explanations of inequality and are quite uncritical of the fact that these are principally cultural definitions. Even the references to the physically and mentally handicapped consistently fail to distinguish between physical disabilities and culturally defined handicaps, so that they too become gross oversimplifications of complex interrelationships and are reduced to clinical categories of people exhibiting 'special needs' and requiring 'special provision'.[32]

In their investigations designed to examine the labelling of Black underachievement in America as pathological, Stephen and Joan Baratz were forced to conclude that 'the social pathology model has led social scientists to establish programmes to prevent deficits which are simply not there'.[33] Black American behaviour, according to their research findings, was not deficit but different. The differentiation arose because of socio-economic circumstances in which certain forms of cultural behaviour were rated differently to others, and in which the behaviour patterns of the poor and powerless were considered to be inferior. The corollary to this assessment, of course, is the assumption that those who are not generally labelled disadvantaged, namely the middle class, exhibit behaviour patterns that are measurably superior. But as Keddie points out, 'models of the good home, etc, when critically examined, are likely to rely on moral imperatives that derive from culture-bound experiences which are presented as given', and determined within the context of a mainstream culture which celebrates the middle-class view of normality and reality.[34]

Bernstein also sees explanations of deprivation and disadvantage as being fixed by a particular view of working-class culture. Theproblem lies in the extent to which definitions of disadvantage are imposed upon one group by another more powerful group. Cole and Bruner make the same point, but in a slightly different context:

Cultural deprivation represents a special case of cultural difference which arises when an individual is faced with demands to perform in a manner inconsistent with his past [cultural] experience. In thepresent social context of the USA [and this is also true of the UK] the great power of the middle class

*has rendered differences into deficits because middle-class behaviour is the
yardstick of success.*[35]

The point of all this is not to suggest that disadvantage does not exist. In structural
terms, inequality of opportunity, of influence, of social and political power and of
economic resources are clearly embedded in the class system. It is the use of the term
to stand for 'personal deficiency' which has to be questioned. The great value of the
arguments presented to challenge deficit and pathological explantions of disadvantage
has been to attack the assumptions on which they are based, their tendency to associate maladjustment with poverty and to hold vast sections of the population personally responsible for their own misfortunes.

The contribution of writers like Keddie and the others has been 'a useful
reminder in a literate society that the illiterate are not inferior beings and that they
may [actually] be rejecting the skills of literacy as part of a rejection of other aspects
of mainstream culture'.[36] Because they have not as yet responded to adult education
initiatives 'does not mean that they are educationally sub-normal or inadequate as
people; many are intellectual and highly articulate, often with well developed practical and social skills'.[37] And the notion that cultural deficit is essentially the creation
of those adhering to the values of mainstream culture is an important antidote to the
rooting of 'disadvantage' in explanations of deviance. But merely to replace theories
of cultural deficit with theories of cultural difference, and to suggest that in a pluralistic
kind of way, a variety of conditions are equally valid, underestimates the social and
economic context within which equality and inequality operate.

The liberal solution

An additional problem so far as adult education is concerned, however, is the
essentially liberal persuasion that underlies its philosophy, and which makes a social
analysis based on notions of cultural hegemony and structural inequality exceedingly
rare.

The associations tied up with the term 'liberal' go much deeper than its more
usual party-political meaning might suggest. It began as a 'specific social distinction,
to refer to a class of free men as distinct from others who were not free'.[38] It came
into the English language in the fourteenth century, and when it was used to refer to
the 'liberal arts' at that time, it was used with social class connotations.

> *The 'liberal arts' were the skills and pursuits appropriate, as we should now
> say, to men of independent means and assured social position, as distinct
> from other [mechanical] skills and pursuits appropriate to a lower class.*[39]

In the eighteenth and nineteenth centuries the term gathered dilettante connotations and the sense of 'open minded' and 'unorthodox' views which has since led to
its disfavour with those of more conservative persuasion. But socialists, and
particularly Marxists, have been even more critical. From their perspective, liberal
ideas seem essentially weak and sentimental and consistently reluctant to take
account of the hard realities of social and economic divisions in society. Certainly in
its historical context, liberalism has been 'a doctrine based on individualist theories

of man and society' and as such 'in fundamental conflict, not only with socialist but [also] with social theories'.[40] The further observation that liberalism is the philosophy most commonly associated with the views of dominant groups in bourgeois society underlines the contradictions between its 'liberating' and 'limiting' ideas of human behaviour – that people should be free to do what they want, unimpeded by too much state interference, just so long as their behaviour doesn't challenge the prevailing distribution of power and influence. In capitalist terms, therefore, liberalism is essentially a doctrine of 'possessive individualism'.[41]

Adult education, with its roots firmly in the nineteenth century, has been part of the trend associated with the progressive enlightenment of an industrial society. Partly initiated by philanthropists, industrialists and liberal academics as a way of civilising the masses, and partly struggled for by those who regarded it as a tool of self improvement it has become both the means of self-fulfilment, and like education generally, a source of enlightenment and reason, dedicated to the development of useful and contented citizens. From the liberal standpoint, adult education can both enhance the quality of individual life and disseminate useful and socially valued knowledge to a limitless range of people, so long as they recognise its intrinsic value. As Bowles and Gintis point out, the liberal view of education creates a belief that education provides the means of furthering personal benefit and fulfilment, whilst at the same time promoting social justice, equality and the integration of the diverse interests of different groups in society.[42]

The assumptions underlying the New Communities Project in Leigh Park in Hampshire, for example, were a celebration of the liberal view of society.[43] The action research team based in a predominantly working-class neighbourhood was clear that 'class solidarity' with the local people would be 'self defeating, unnecessary and perhaps distorting. . . If the whole of our cultural heritage should be available to the working class, then education for individual self discovery and self development' should be the starting point. The team's conclusions were that if education 'begins where people are' and aims to 'encourage growth in human personality, character and creativity' and provides space in which to develop 'greater confidence in their own ability and potential' then 'trends in adult education during this century (towards the monopolisation of provision by middle-class groups) will be arrested and the balance of opportunity may swing to a more central position.'

This sense of optimistic progressivism has been a feature of liberal adult education since its inception. It provided the enthusiasm which once established and developed tutorial classes and identified a curriculum considered to represent the highest and most worthy forms of thought then known to human beings. It has informed and fostered the national literacy campaign, and the sentiments for notions of continuing education, community education and life-long learning.

During the last ten years or so, however, there has been a fair amount of criticism of the liberal position – largely in terms of its naivety and lack of critical social awareness. In America writers like Illich, Reimer, Postman and Weingartner, among others, have challenged the whole notion of education as an enlightened and liberating experience. The brunt of their critique is made against the alienating procedures of schooling, but it is the process of manufactured education which they are criticising, and as such, much of what they say is equally applicable to adult education. Prepackaged courses and inflexible procedures bedevil much of the provision and despite the rhetoric of 'student-centredness', in a feepaying, enrolment economy, they are readily reduced to statistics. In its recent report, *A Strategy for the Basic Education of Adults*, the committee set up by the Advisory Council for Adult and Continuing Education and chaired by Henry Arthur Jones chose surprisingly mechanistic language to describe a procedure in which:

> *a tutor or organiser is likely to spend several hours* **on** *an intending student* (**case discussion** *with the* **referring agent, diagnostic** *and advisory interviews with* **briefing** *the prospective tutor) before the student becomes, if he ever does, a* **statistic on an enrolment card.** *[my emphasis]*[44]

For the deschoolers educational institutions are essentially repressive organisations which peddle a commodity-based view of knowledge, and which measure success and failure in terms of procedures and values which are meaningless to the vast majority of potential students. As such their claims about 'concern for the individual' appear to be particularly hypocritical.

A rather different kind of challenge to liberal ideas in education has come from social economists like Bowles and Gintis, who argue that even in its own terms, liberalism has not fulfilled the expectations which it has created. Their examples of the bankruptcy of American attempts to combat social and educational disadvantage can be parallelled by similar futilities in Britain. Despite Urban Aid, community education, community development, positive discrimination in Educational Priority Areas, the national literacy campaign and a proliferation of long-term and short-term action research projects, all designed to provide new opportunities for the disadvantaged, there is no evidence to suggest that the poverty we rediscovered in the 1960s, and which we have now added to by structural unemployment, has in any way subsided. In retrospect, most of these initiatives seem to have been essentially the piecemeal and pragmatic responses to externally defined local problems, and sustained briefly by virtue of the inordinate energy of exceptional and highly motivated individuals. Experts with minimal resources found that their ability to effect change was limited. So long as they were there, however, the appearance of 'something being done' was sufficient to harness the enthusiasm of new recruits to the liberal cause.

Unfortunately, as in America, there is now some suggestion that the liberal reform bubble has burst. In political as much as in intellectual circles, the current mood is one of 'retrenchment.'[45] But the weakness of liberalism generally, and liberal views about educational needs, is more fundamental than the 'temporary setback' accounted for by a change of government or the 'short term effects' of an international recession.

As Bowles and Gintis point out, the central weakness of the liberal view of education and society is that it leaves unquestioned the economic and political structure in society, in which the creation of disadvantage occurs, and in which educational reforms are expected to operate. In a society like Britain, the existence of a capitalist economy, the social class divisions created as a consequence of it, and the contribution made to its preservation and reproduction by the education system, render liberal aspirations based on 'spiritual fulfilment', 'personhood'[46] and 'social integration' impossible to achieve. The likelihood of conditions like these, whatever they actually mean, becoming generally accepted, seems totally unrealistic when they are examined in terms of an education system which exists to deny anything but marginal modifications in the prevailing distribution of resources in society. The liberal hope of changing the context and process of education to make it more responsive to the needs of the disadvantaged is a vain one without corresponding and significant changes in the organisation and control of economic life.

The suggestion that adult education should tackle this problem alone is, of course, rarely advocated. But the view that adult education can play a corrective role in co-operation with other professional and voluntary agencies is a familiar plank in the liberal platform. So far as education for the disadvantaged is concerned, Russell gave the seal of approval to inter-agency co-operation as a key strategy in its development, and much discussion about the 'grey area' between education and social work has informed a good deal of recent thinking on the matter.[47]

But of course the contradictions affecting the liberal position in education are just as apparent in the other, so-called 'caring professions' of social, health and welfare services. Their responsibilities demand thatthey address themselves to relieving the deprivation, alienation and inequalities which accompany the prevailing economic practice of capitalism, dedicating themselves to the general enhancement of human development and fulfilment. The extent to which members of the welfare professions deliberately conspire with others to perpetuate false expectations is, of course, not the charge being made. But by subscribing to the collective delusion of short-sighted liberal optimism, they leave unquestioned the deep rooted political and economic structures which make their aims impossible to achieve.

In addition, their naivety and energy serve as excellent methods of social control. Their benevolence and sense of vocation encourage them to work harder than they are paid to do, and their reputation for being 'good people' neutralises the hostility of their 'clients' and renders objectionable, subversive, or jaundiced the challenges of their critics.

Their achievement is to socialise their clients into what Smith and Harris refer to as 'ideologies of need'. Rather like a self-fulfilling prophecy, they create 'states of awareness' from which people develop both the symptoms and the frames of reference which make the diagnoses of their deviant behaviour seem perfectly plausible.[48] Illich argues that the capacity of 'welfare bureaucracies (to) claim a professional, political and financial manipulation over the social imagination, to define the needs and problems of the clients, and to set the standards of what is valuable and feasible' makes them 'addictive'.[49] Their language and quasi-medical terminology not only mystifies their expertise but reinforces their authority as agents of social control.

In comparison to all the literature dedicated to the rehabilitation of social deviants, it is refreshing to read Jenny Headlam Wells's contention that 'a *person's failure* to "adjust" to disability may be interpreted as a positive sign, indicating a refusal to accept the patronising, infantilising and passive role that our society tends to ascribe to the disabled.'[50] But her opinion is the exception rather than the rule.

It would be unusual to expect the welfare professions and the work they do to be anything other than reformist, however. In many cases their origins are recent. They lack the corporate identity and exclusivity of the older professions, but by the careful expansion of training and professionalisation over the last thirty years or so, they have steadily extended their realm of influence, until together, they have become increasingly responsible for the assessment and treatment of behaviour in many areas of social life.

These are groups who have acquired social legitimacy as 'experts', and in the process of their professionalisation, they have become adopted as professional experts by the state and local government, operating from a respected and privileged social position. A good deal of authority is accredited to their judgements, so that collectively they are encouraged to identify and service the needs of an entire population according to *their* interpretations of reality. Economic and political questions are translated into individual and technical problems, and as such, they have disguised the extent to which they are engaged in a highly important and supremely political range of activities.

For adult education to combine with these agencies in the identification of needs and the provision of programmes for those considered to be disadvantaged, there is a real danger that welfare therapy and the central ideology which typifies its professional position, will emerge as the predominant characteristic of educational programmes – programmes which should be essentially different kinds of activities. Clearly, then, in an attempt to assess the initiatives intended to respond to the needs of the disadvantaged, it is important to be clear that there are different ideological assumptions at work and different explanations of the causes and characteristics of disadvantage, Inevitably both of these cultural preconditions influence the aims and objectives, the curriculum and pedagogy and the evaluation of the activities which are offered.

In this respect Colin Fletcher's distinction between liberal and liberating interpretations of community education is crucial[51] as is Thomas La Belle's distinction between a 'deprivation-development' and a 'dependency-liberation' classification of education and social change in the Third World.[52] La Belle is referring to strategies of development in developing countries. He contrasts interpretations of society which equate educational disadvantage with pathological explanations of human deficit (i.e. deprivation) and those which explain disadvantage as a consequence of structural inequalities that keep powerless groups in a state of dependency on the economic and cultural decisions made by ruling groups. Strategies to deal with deprivation, in La Belle's first typology, employ remediation, compensatory education, training and behaviour modification (development). Those which seek to challenge and transform the relationship of dependency described in his second model are those which set out to enhance the authority and power of the disadvantaged in relation to the dominant group. To promote liberation in fact. But 'liberation' may seem a bit strong when transferred to the British context of adult education. Freire's equally committed language of 'conscientisation' and the like is more palatable –

largely, I suspect, because his views have become a part of the content of the academic study of adult education, much as the ideas of Illich and the deschoolers became part of the curriculum of every respectably progressive teacher-training establishment in the early 1970s. So long as their ideas seem to be interesting, but of no direct relevance to educational practice in this country, they can be incorporated in the curriculum, and discussed in abstraction, without seriously challenging the behaviour and practice of the institutions involved.

But La Belle's notion of liberation is an important one to take up within the context of British adult education because there *is* a different set of assumptions and explanations about what adult education should be about in relation to the disadvantaged. It is largely a minority view, for obvious reasons, but it's a view which needs to be put with increasing vigour if educational opportunities for working-class men and women are to advance much further.

Adult education and the working class

Critical educational theorists of all types – from Althusser to Bowles and Gintis – have agreed that education is one of the most important (if not the most important) institution by which ruling groups, in western society, establish and maintain their hegemony and reproduce the conditions of capitalist production.

The problem is to relate the theoretical arguments of Althusser, Gramsci, Bowles and Gintis, Freire, the deschoolers and all the rest to understanding everyday educational experience, and especially adult education in which the legacy of unquestioned liberalism is perhaps most complacent. To begin with, none of these theorists is British. Their theories were developed in different cultural, historical and social circumstances. In reaching Britain they have become separated from their original political contexts. The links between these theoretical perspectives and British educational practice still have to be made.

A second problem relates to the demarcation between theory and practice in British adult education. Colin Kirkwood argues that:

> practitioners are out in the field, taken up with teaching (if they are lucky),
> organising and administrating the provision. Most theorists, on the other
> hand, live and work in academic worlds remote from those of fieldwork
> practice. Much British adult education theory is bland, latinate,
> unilluminating. For insight and regeneration of the world of practice it
> substitutes . . . rationales for the existing pattern of practice. When
> fieldworkers enter the debate, it is not to contribute at a conceptual or
> theoretical level but merely to give accounts of their practice.[53]

Keith Jackson makes a similar point in his scepticism about a good many action research projects which so frequently provide a 'post-hoc eulogy of whatever happened to happen 'without much attention to theory.[54]

A third problem is the contradictory tendencies of those political groups in Britain which exist to represent working-class interests.

> Historically the British working class has been at the forefront of the struggle
> for state education – ever since the Knowledge Chartists argued that
> education could be an important counter to the raw exploitation of working
> class children by an unrestrained labour market.[55]

The Labour movement, the Labour Party and the Communist Party have all seen education as a potential weapon with which to resist the exploitation of workers by employers. All of the developments in state education during the last hundred years or so have been to some extent the consequence of pressure for equality of educational opportunity for working-class people demanded by their representatives. The tension between the provision of education by the state as a means of social differentiation and control, as against the demand for education by the working class as a way of transforming its situation, has been a continuing conflict both in schooling and in the provision of adult education. Corrigan and Frith describe the history of British education as:

> a reluctant bourgeoisie slowly yielding to socialist and working-class demands
> for general schooling, secondary education for all, the expansion of higher
> education, comprehensive schools and the raising of the school leaving age.[56]

But all of these developments, as we have seen, distract attention from deeper considerations about the role of education. Within the general expansion of educational opportunity, and the shift towards more comprehensive provision at all levels, rarely have questions been raised by the working class or its representatives about the content or control of these facilities.

The critical arguments advanced by the theorists about the education system and its relation to society are all part of a genuine attempt to change that society. But the difficulty is one of relating the theory to everyday practice, and one of relating changes in educational institutions to the class struggle generally, especially within the context of social and ideological structures which are very powerful and highly resistant to change.

The libertarian solution of the deschoolers is to disestablish the professions and deinstitutionalise society on behalf of individual freedom. But this much vaunted individualism does not have much relevance to the conditions of the working class generally and, as some would argue, makes it 'more akin to the right wing, laissez-faire approach of the "educational voucher" Tories'.[57]

The Midwinter solution, based on recommendations about curriculum relevance, enjoyed initial support in the late 1960s and early 1970s because it appeared to celebrate cultural difference as a positive alternative to the denigratory notions of cultural deficit. The same call for relevance has been a popular feature of adult education developments in working-class areas and with groups considered to be socially disadvantaged. But the identification of relevance as an objective begs the important question of whose definition is being advanced? Critics of the relevancy and relativist view of knowledge warn of the danger of locking working-class people into a limited and parochial view of the world, and depriving them of the forms of knowledge they need if they are to transform their social and economic situations[58] Martin

Yarnit, from a totally different political perspective, has the same reservations about Midwinter's restrictive use of the concept of social relevance.[59] Traditional knowledge is not 'of itself ' repressive; it is made to be repressive through the processes of certification, specialisation, monopolisation and control used by ruling groups in society, seeking to maintain their cultural hegemony over the others.

> *To limit access to this heritage on the grounds that its relevance to working-class men and women is not immediately apparent is, in effect,to perpetuate the system which creates this irrelevancy. It is to concede defeat without even attempting to win: it is to institutionalise the exploitation and alienation experienced by the working class as consumers as well as producers, in the cultural and educational sphere.[60]*

A fourth problem is that, just as an increasing number of working-class children respond to their schooling with apathy, boredom, indiscipline and truancy, working-class men and women seem to be visibly unattracted to adult education for the countless reasons that prevent it being seen as useful, interesting or exciting to them. Their apparent resistance lends great weight to the views which depict their 'indifference', 'residual hostility to education' and general lack of appreciation of the 'finer things of life' as symptomatic of their 'cultural deficiency'. But again, as Keith Jackson and Bob Ashcroft point out, because the ruling class has profound cultural supremacy,

> *in addition to control over the means of production and its accompanying coercive apparatus, the dominant class [also] exercises crucial control over the apparatus of cultural dissemination (institutions of learning, the arts, the mass media) in short over all those means through which social consciousness could be effectively created. Without resorting to the contentious notion of false consciousness, ruling class cultural hegemony can be seen as giving the working class no effective choice between alternatives. Without wishing to question the consumption choices themselves, of material goods and leisure pursuits by the working class . . . [it is important] to question the milieu in which these choices are made. This milieu is essentially one of constraint and manipulation [which] emerges from a social structure which in the most extreme form limits theoptions open to the working class and expands those open to the middle class, [my emphases][61]*

In such circumstances, the relative disinterest shown by working class men and women to adult education, working-class politics, literature and social history, for example, compared to their concern for other commercial and leisure pursuits, is a measure of the success of the ruling class's contribution to the creation of working-class counter-consciousness.

Frith and Corrigan's conclusion is that

> *state education is a good thing as a source of skills necessary for the working class to resist the brutalising effects of the market; state education is a bad thingas an instrument of bourgeois domination . . . these contradictions reflect the contradictions within capitalism itself . . . in the long run the*

contradictions will only be solved by thetransformation of capitalist relations
in general, but the immediate problem of educational policy is a tactical one:
how caneducational systems become a part of the struggle for socialism?[62]

So far as working-class adult education is concerned, does the politics of education mean gaining control of existing institutions on behalf of working-class students in the universities, the WEA and local authority classes? Or does it mean creating independent socialist institutions as the Plebs League tried to do in 1909, and more recently, the Southern Region Trade Union Information and Research Unit has tried to do in reaction to the industrial studies policies of Southampton University?[63]

Underlying all of these questions is the problem of the relationship between education and society and the extent to which significant changes in the provision of education can be achieved without major social and economic changes in the wider society. Paradoxically, though, it is precisely because the education system is a reflection of the vested interests, social values and economic concerns of dominant groups in capitalist society that it provides the setting in which the contradictions of the class struggle can be made explicit. The conflicts and struggles apparent within the education system reflect the conflicts and struggles of the wider society. By exposing these and re-examining them in political terms, it is possible to make clear to the teachers, tutors and students involved, the implications of the process and procedures in which they are caught up. Conscientisation is a crucial first step. The fusion of critical awareness, social action and reflection upon action through praxis is consequently an important socialist response to the issues raised in this paper so far.

No wonder it is a minority view! It's a response in favour of the definition of 'disadvantage' being made in class terms, the provision of educational activities which take seriously the social condition and educational development of working-class men and women, and a political commitment to their class interests as concerns which are very different to middle-class interests. This means placing adult education for the working class very specifically in the wider context of political struggle, and to ensure, as the students of Barbiana demanded, that educational means are never isolated from political ends.[64]

Illustrations of this kind of adult education for working-class men and women in contemporary Britain are, for obvious reasons, not easy to find. But for those who are attempting to relate their practice to a realistic assessment of the structural repercussions of a class based society, the work of Tom Lovett in Northern Ireland, and in a different context, Keith Jackson and his colleagues in Liverpool, has obviously been an important influence.[65]

Like many activists, Jackson's writing has not always kept pace with his activities, and it is to the earlier articles produced with Bob Ashcroft, and to relatively obscure conference papers, that we must turn for inspiration. To repeat Jackson and Ashcroft's commitment to a clear theoretical framework as a guide to practice, and their recognition of the specific values and interests which education serves in society, would be to reinforce the arguments already outlined in this paper. Their important additional contributions to the debate are in three main areas.

The first seems to me to be the fearless and specific use of class terminology in relation to adult students and educational practice. There are parts of the country – and Southampton is one of them – where the definition of 'working class' is seen as both pejorative and divisive. It is also, paradoxically, seen by many to be both patronising and irrelevant in terms of adult education provision. For Jackson and Ashcroft there are no such problems – nor for the students referred to by David Evans and Martin Yarnit either, I suspect,[66] But whilst the softer south disguises some of the more visible manifestations of class difference and class inequality, the relative mal-distribution of resources is no less true in areas like these. The resistance to attempts to make them explicit and part of the process of education and conscientisation is strong in an area which has been sheltered to some extent from the worst excesses of industrial and economic dislocation. Relative affluence has allowed the conviction that 'we are all middle class now' to dig deeper into the social fabric, and to distract both the middle and working class from many of the face-to-face realities of urban decay and structural unemployment. But whilst Leigh Park, central Southampton or down-town Portsmouth might seem like 'paradise' compared to Scotland Road, many of the houses still have black damp, there are still minimal social amenities, high rates of youth unemployment and a local stigma attached to living there. Their residents are still those who are most vulnerable to economic crisis and least well served by the education, health and welfare services, and their adult residents are just as unlikely as working-class men and women anywhere to find their way into adult education classes which reflect any understanding or concern about their situation.

However unpalatable it may be to some people, the concept of social class is a much more appropriate one in which to discuss educational opportunities than those of 'personhood', 'disadvantage' or 'deprivation', precisely because it places the discussion firmly in the context of a stratified society in which middle-class interests determine the parameters within which the education system operates. It also allows the application of terms commonly understood in 'sociological' as distinct from 'social problem' analysis to be used.

Jackson has distinguished between two broad definitions of working class.[67] The first definition concentrates on

> an aggregate of low status individuals . . . whose low status is defined by
> social and economic criteria: employment (or lack of it), income, educational
> background, job opportunities, general access to resources indicated by area
> of residence, ability to choose residence, lifestyle, etc.

The majority of the various groups already referred to as 'disadvantaged' in liberal terminology would come within this definition of working-class.

The second definition is of a group who share the social and economic conditions described above but who have a 'degree of consciousness' about their position. In this sense the concept working-class takes on more active and positive connotations. Jackson describes this understanding of being working class as one of 'being involved in a social, economic and political relationship, varying according to personality and experience. It entails belonging to a social class not a category'. Each of these definitions has different implications for educational action, thus Jackson and Ashcroft's second contribution is to challenge their potential divisiveness, especially when they are further qualified by notions of 'working class affluence' and the 'culture of deprivation'. They argue quite rightly that 'the similarities between the social experiences of the "deprived" and "affluent" working class are much more important than the differences'. To concentrate on 'the deprived', however half-hearted and ineffective that concentration turns out to be, puts the emphasis on neighbourhood consciousness rather than class consciousness. It sets one neighbourhood against the other in competition for scarce resources and one deprived group's 'positive discrimination' becomes another's 'economic restriction'. It replaces the strength of class consciousness and the recognition of class conflict by the less abrasive and more malleable notion of 'community development'. It helps explain why affluent workers in less critically deprived areas feel little or no allegiance with working people in other areas. And why the desperation of poverty, unemployment and poor housing conditions can easily be converted into the acceptance of racialist and materialistic propaganda – the effective modern solution to the old concern to 'divide and rule'. The concept of deprivation or disadvantage, therefore, is not appropriate unless it is extended to cover the position of the whole working class, whether poor or not, and used to demonstrate the links between their common powerlessness in comparison to others in contemporary society.

Their third contribution is the emphasis on work with activists and the recognition that well-informed, politically conscious and influential activists have a much greater social and political influence among their neighbours and workmates than others working from a strictly educational base. The account of the 'Second Chance to Learn' course in *Adult Education for a Change* describes developments which are to some extent the consequence of having taken the decision to work with activists as far as possible in Liverpool. In these terms even small resources put into trade union education or educational work with 'natural' as distinct from 'elected' leaders can have a much more important multiplier effect than the same resources used in the school system. And if the definition of 'skill' and 'resource' is wide enough to encompass other forms of working-class cultural expression, then broadsheets, drama, radio, TV and poetry, for example, can all be used to reflect and inform working-class action.[68]

Central to all of this, of course, is the element of equality and common interest implicit in the term 'solidarity'. It is this demonstration of 'solidarity' that is so frequently missing from philosophies of adult education which 'treat' students as 'disadvantaged', philosophies which imply that there are two clear sides to the relationship. 'Those with the needs, mindless incompetents, on the one hand, and the need-meeters on the other, perceptive, enquiring, responsible, able to take a broad view and make prescriptions'.[69] Rather, the relationship between teachers and students should be built upon the demonstration of solidarity and on principles of equality and genuine mutual respect.

In practice all of this means believing that education is a dialogue in which the teachers must be as ready to learn as the potential students. The point is well made in Paul Thompson's book, *The Voice of the Past*, in which he describes the oral historian of working-class history as one coming to listen, *to sit at the feet of others who, because they come from a different social class, or are less educated, or older, know more about something. The reconstruction of history itself becomes a much more widely collaborative process, in which 'non-professionals' mustplay a crucial part.*[70]

In education the dialogue should begin with the issues chosen by the student and not the teacher. Since 'education for its own sake' is rarely a luxury that working-class men and women can afford, these issues will be largely instrumental – concerned with welfare rights, employment, housing, etc. The responsibility of the teacher is to try to develop the discussion beyond the boundaries of the already known, and into the area of the unknown, which still has to be discovered, understood, mastered and controlled by the students. This will mean making the kind of intellectual demands upon working-class men and women that are properly made on all students.

By comparison, the limitations built into the notions of 'functional literacy', 'role education', 'coping skills' and 'basic education' generally all serve to reinforce the restricted expectations that teachers frequently have of those labelled 'disadvantaged'. The limited expectations are reinforced by the psychological explanations which underlie them and which assume that the motivation to learn is personal. As Freire, Bowles and Gintis, the deschoolers and the others have demonstrated, however, low motivation and lack of achievement are closely related to the alienating experiences of the educational system dominated by hierarchical social relations. If the educational process is based on a mutual dialogue which sets out to incorporate the class interests of working people into its operations, then the opportunities to learn become quite different and are based on a different set of relationships and assumptions. If, as Keith Jackson and Bob Ashcroft argue, education is 'directly concerned with consciousnesss and awareness in class terms, the form of the educational dialogue can closely relate motivation, the concept of learning and its cultural matrix'.[71] Although uncommon in Britain, this is essentially the approach which has been used with some success in Latin America.

The use of 'social class' as distinct from 'disadvantage' as the conceptual base from which to operate poses a number of problems for those engaged in adult education, however, just as it did for those employed by the Home Office and local authorities in the CDPS. It's difficult to imagine any circumstances in which this kind of work could ever become a regular part of conventional adult education.

Those of us involved have obviously learned by experience where the institutional boundaries lie. Clearly there is no problem, or very little problem, expressing solidarity with illiterates, the handicapped, the elderly, or in developing community links with a mothers and toddlers group or a parent-teacher association. But when a group, conscious of its working-class interests, wishes to use the normal democratic procedures in society and bring them into the curriculum of adult education, then there are problems. Such boundaries mark out quite clearly the real limitations on the popular rhetoric of 'relevance' and 'responding to felt needs' so beloved by adult education practitioners.

The counter-arguments employed by our colleagues are well known. They point to the elitism of the Ruskin-type tradition, which they argue elevates bright working-class people into the middle class and away from their roots. And clearly they are right. Some working-class adults will use education as a means of escaping from the social and economic limitations of their previous experience. But 'learning' as such does not necessarily need to be a synonym for self-improvement. If education is initially related to 'consciousness', then learning becomes a 'social' as distinct from a purely 'personal' activity. For other critics, education for social awareness is 'a recipe for resentment' and 'a formula for frustration'. It is considered wrong to 'raise people's expectations' when nothing can be changed. This argument also hits home. Those who are made aware of their impotence by education are clearly in a difficult position. The prevailing social structure would also be better served if they were left in ignorance. But if working-class men and women come to see more clearly, and to understand the extent and the range of the restrictions imposed upon them, then they are in a better position to do something about them. Critical awareness is the essential prerequisite for the determined action necessary to alter such restrictions.

In either argument the liberal tradition in adult education ideas finds its justification for keeping things much as they are. But if inequality is indeed the social context in which education operates, then to do nothing, or to resort to pious declarations of concern for the 'hidden and largely defeated population whom life has taught to keep their heads down and not expect much'[72] is to perpetuate the system which orchestrates their defeat.

The third counter-argument is simple. It is that views like these are held by 'politically motivated activists', 'committed to creating class conflict' where it does not exist and relentlessly ignoring 'the freedom of individuals' to 'live as they choose'. But of course the simple is also the simplistic. The commitment to working-class adult education, and the recognition of conditions which positively reinforce working class culture on the one hand, and negatively restrict working-class opportunities on the other, is not a stand any of those involved in such practice would wish to deny.

More serious is the denial of the ideology which is not made explicit in the philosophy and practice of adult education generally, and adult education for the disadvantaged in particular. It is this 'hidden' ideology which really imposes on working-class men and women; perpetually determining, and yet repeatedly disclaiming any responsibility for, their defeat.

Notes and References

1.   Michael Rutter and Nicola Madge (eds), *Cycles of Disadvantage* (Heinemann, 1976)
2.   John Bowlby, *Maternal Care and Mental Health* (WHO, 1951)
3.   L. Casler, *Maternal Deprivation: A Critical Review of the Literature*, Monograph of the Society for Research into Child Development, no 26 (1961)
4.   W.G. Runciman, *Relative Deprivation and Social Justice*
5.   B. Ekland and D.P. Kent, Socialisation and Social Structure', in *Perspectives on Human Deprivation: Biological, Psychological and Social* (UD Dept. of Health and Education and Welfare, 1968)
6.   H. Ginsberg, *The Myth of the Deprived Child* (Prentice Hall, 1972); and Norman Freidman,

Cultural Deprivation; a Commentary in the Sociology of Knowledge, *Journal of Educational Thought*, vol no 2 (1967)

7. M.D. Ashworth, The Effects of Maternal Deprivation: A Review of Findings and Controversy in the Context of Research Strategy, in *Deprivation of Mental Care: A Reassessment of its Effects* (WHO 1962)

8. Rutter and Madge, *Cycles of Disadvantage.*

9. Jim Callaghan. Home Secretary, Introduction to the Urban Aid Programme, *Hansard* (2 December 1968).

10. Home Office Press Release (16 July 1969)

11. Coventry CDP Final Report, Part 1 (1975)

12. i.e. *Oxford and Working Class Education*, 1908: *The Final Report of the Adult Education Committee of the Ministry of Reconstruction*, 1919; *The Ashby Report*, 1954; and *The Russell Report*, 1973.

13. E and E Hutchinson, *Learning Later* (Routledge and Kegan Paul, 1978).

14. H.A. Jones in his foreword to Peter Clyne, *The Disadvantaged Adult* (Longman, 1972).

15. H.A. Jones, ibid.

16. H.A. Jones, ibid.

17. Peter Clyne, ibid.

18. See, for example, The recommendations made as a consequence of the New Communities Project in Leigh Park and outlined in Fordham, Poulton and Randle, (Routledge and Kegan Paul, 1979).

19. The ACACE Report A Strategy for the Basic Education of Adults, 1979, also supervised by Henry Arthur Jones with Clyne as a committee member, was more obliged than Russell had been to take account of the economic crisis and escalating unemployment of the mid 70s. But the emphasis in this report is still essentially on personal inadequacy in circumstances in which structural unemployment and redundancy, however distressing, are taken as 'given' and with solutions seen to lie in 'coping skills' and 'basic education available wherever needed to *counter* the loss of perperonal dignity, the waste of human resources and the *vulnerability to political extremism* that hopeless unemployment can bring' (my italics).

20. K.H. Lawson, Community Education: A Critical Assessment, *Adult Education*, vol. 50, no1.

21. Graham Mee and Harold Wiltshire, *Structure and Performance in Adult Education*, (Longman, 1978).

22. Keith Jackson, Adult Education and Social Action, Jones and Mayo (eds) *Community Work One* (Routledge and Kegan Paul)

23. See Friedman, *Cultural Deprivation* op cit.

24. Christopher Jencks, Johnson vs Poverty, *New Republic*, no 150 (1964).

25. Jencks in the *Moynihan Report* (1965).

26. Norman friedman, *Cultural deprivation*, op cit.

27. Basil Bernstein, Education Cannot Compensate for Society, *New Society*, (26 February 1970).

28. 'Mainstream culture' is a term which writers like Keddie have utilised to refer to the dominance of middle class cultural values.

29. Kenneth Clark, *Dark Ghetto: Dilemmas of Social Power* (1965).

30. Bernstein, Education Cannot Compensate for Society.

31. William Ryan, Savage Discovery, in *the Moynihan Report* (1965).

32. Jenny Headlam Wells, Adult Education and Disadvantage: the Special Needs of Physically Handicapped Students, *Adult Education*, vol 49, no 6.

33. Baratz and Baratz, *Early Childhood Intervention: The Social Science of Institutional Racism* (1970).
34. Nell Keddie, Social Differentiation (2)Unit 10, E 282. (Open University)
35. Cole and Bruner, *Preliminaries to a Theory of Cultural Difference* (1972).
36. Giles and Woolf, units 25 and 26, E 202 (Open University).
37. Introduction and Guide to Reading Development PE 231 (Open University)
38. Raymond Williams in *Keywords* (Fontana 1976)
39. ibid.
40. ibid.
41. ibid.
42. Herbert Bowles and Samuel Gintis, *Schooling in Capitalist America* (Routledge and Kegan Paul, 1976).
43. Fordham, Poulton and Randle, *Learning Networks in Adult Education.*
44. *A Strategy for the Basic Education of Adults,* para 70.
45. Bowles and Gintis, op cit.
46. See R.W.K. Paterson, *Values, Education and the Adult,* (Routledge and Kegan Paul, 1979).
47. Fordham, Poulton and Randle, op cit.
48. Smith and Harris, Ideologies of Need and the Organisation of Social Work Departments, *British Journal of Social Work,* vol 12, no.1.
49. Ivan Illich, *Deschooling Society* (Penguin, 1973).
50. Jenny Headlam Wells, op cit.
51. Colin Fletcher, Chapter 3. *Adult Education for a Change,* (ed) Jane Thompson (Hutchinson, 1980).
52. Thomas la Belle, Goals and Strategies of Non Formal Education in Latin America, in *Comparitive Education Review,* vol 20, no 3.
53. Colin Kirkwood, Adult Education and the Concept of Community, *Adult Education,* vol 51, no 3.
54. Keith Jackson, *Adult Education in a Community Development Project,* (1973)
55. Simon Frith and Paul Corrigan, The Politics of Education, Geoff Whitty and M F D Young, in *Society, State and Schooling,* (Falmer Press, 1977).
56. ibid.
57. ibid., and Guy Neaves' article The Free Schoolers in Douglas Holly (ed) *Education for Domination,* (Arrow Books, 1974).
58. See, for example, Richard Pring, Knowledge Out of Control, *Education for Teaching,* (November, 1971); Jim Campbell and Martin Merson, Community Education: Instruction for Inequality, *Education for Teaching* (Spring 1974); and John and Pat White, Slogan for Crypto- Elitists?, in *TES* (5 January 1973).
59. Martin Yarnit, Chapter 9, *Adult Education for a Change.*
60. Keith Jackson and Bob Ashcroft, *Adult Education, Deprivation and Community Development – A Critique,* (1972).
61. ibid.
62. Frith and Corrigan, *The Politics of Education.*
63. In October 1978, Basil Bye, Lecturer in Industrial Relations at Southampton University resigned his post. During the preceding 12 years, together with local shop stewards and regional trade union officials he had helped to establish the Southern Region *Trade Union Information and Research Unit.* At first this organisation worked in close co-operation with the university, as it did with the WEA, the TUC and individual trade unions. Increasingly it was felt that the university's definition of 'liberal adult education' was being used to imply an unacceptable bias in the work of the Industrial Studies Unit. The

SRTUIRU felt under sufficient restriction to declare its independence from the university connection. It now operates independently but in close harmony with the TUC and individual unions. Its work is flourishing. The university's provision of trade union education, on the other hand, is, at the time of writing (July 1979), now confined to three part-time certificate courses in Industrial relations which draws students from both sides of industry.

64. School of Barbiana, *Letter to a Teacher*, (Penguin, 1970).
65. See Chapter 8 by Tom Lovett, *Adult Education for a Change*. Keith Jackson is now Senior Tutor at the Northern College, Barnsley.
66. See chapters 7 and 9 in *Adult Education for a Change*.
67. Keith Jackson, ' Notes on the background to the appointment of an action researcher in adult education for a working class neighbourhood', University of Liverpool, internal paper.
68. David Evans, Chapter 7 in *Adult Education for a Change*.
69. Colin Kirkwood, op cit.
70. Paul Thompson, *The Voice of the Past: Oral History*, (Opus 1978).
71. Jackson and Ashcroft, *Adult Education, Deprivation and Community Development*.
72. *A Strategy for the Basic Education of Adults* (ACACE 1979).

The personal implications of women's subordination

(Originally published in *Learning Liberation:*
Women's Response to Men's Education,
Jane Thompson, Croom Helm, 1983)

Deriving from the energy and critical theory of second wave feminism during the seventies and early eighties **Learning Liberation: Women's Response to Men's Education** *was one of the first publications in the recent history of adult and continuing education to look at the widespread domination of a predominantly women's service by malestream ideas and men's authority. It encouraged women working in the service to take up a feminist stance and helped to validate many of the grass roots and outreach initiatives which were taking place in adult and community education informed by the enthusiasm for feminism. Published in 1983 the book found its way beyond the UK to Ireland, Australia, Canada, the United States, New Zealand and Japan. In this extract Thompson relates the purpose of women's education to the struggle for women's liberation from subordination. She makes use of the feminist conviction that the personal is also political, providing the preliminary information from which to derive theory and to inform action. It is made clear that women understanding their experience constitutes an important ingredient of radical learning and is closely related to the ways in which such politicised education can assist in the process of reflection and consciousness-raising necessary to inform personal and collective action by women for social change.*

The personal implications of women's subordination

Prisoners

Every street, road, village, town has them, Small dots at windows.
Watching, waiting patiently
For escape, a chance to be free, Hours turning to days, to weeks,
to months and years.
Lives are wasting,
like stale vegetation.
Chained by guilt,
unable to be free
Somebody must help them before their lives end.
Too late,
More lives lost.

Angela Weaver[1]

Single status in a culture in which marriage is encouraged is not the only form of marginality that women can expect to experience. Although women in Britain actually outnumber men in the population[2], the sense of being as equally as important as men in the organisation and deliberations of the state is not part of women's experience. The history of human endeavour, the concerns of men and the future of mankind are all concepts which we assume embrace women within their frame of reference, but in the process of constructing a grammar which neatly subsumes she within he, and her within him, we have lost sight not only of feminine symbols, but also of female reality and experience.

Elaine Morgan[3] is absolutely right when she says that the prehistory of mankind would reflect very different assumptions about the world if we were to find recorded that 'When the first ancestor of the human race descended from the trees she had not yet developed the mighty brain that was to distinguish her so sharply from other species'.

It is not merely that the English language reflects male experience and male constructs[4], or that the mediation of expertise and the formulation of opinions are controlled and delivered by men[5], but that shared social conditions like work and unemployment, sport and recreation, political activism and unrest all appear as male issues and male concerns.

Somewhere in the presentation of male reality and male perspectives as the totality of human experience, women have ceased to exist in a serious and visible way. Women have become marginal to the general concerns of human existence, which is in fact male existence. Women appear only in sex-specific discussions about, for example, mating and mothering and making ends meet. In matters of general concern the voice of authority is male, and Joe Public is exactly who his masculine name suggests. An important lesson we need to learn as women is to discover how power in the hands of men has been used to determine our marginality, and why we have accepted this position. The words of women I have included here are of course their own, but they carry with them the collective wisdom of countless women who have lived and shared a similar experience.

As we have seen, the concern of schooling is to teach women a salutary lesson – to know their place and to accept it. For many, school has been a meaningless and unpleasant experience in which it was usual to feel marginal, although not always to understand why.

As for schooldays – I don't really remember much about them. I know the secondary modern was vast with hundreds of kids all around. I didn't like it from the start. The teachers didn't seem to care whether you understood what they said. Things were pumped into you – if they stayed in your brain, all well and good, if they didn't, too bad. I never had the courage to question and so I just plodded on and left at 15 – not very bright but not quite a twit. I just hated it all.

I suppose I would be classed as one of the millions of failures. Maybe half of it was my fault. I suppose you would call me a non-conformist. I found it difficult to comply with all those petty rules and regulations and consequently alienated myself from the teachers. They had labelled me as a troublesome pupil. There was no point in working because I knew I couldn't stay on to take exams (I came from a large family and the need to earn a wage was ever present) and I feel that any effort on my part would be wasted anyway. The teaching itself was on the whole uninteresting and boring. There never seemed to be much effort put into the actual enjoyment level of the pupils. The teachers kept themselves apart – they stood at the front of the class and talked 'at' us rather than 'to' us . . . On the whole it was all too formal. The overall feeling was that they were there because it was their job, and we were there because the law stated that we had to be. I left at the age of 15 with no qualifications, labelled by the teachers as 'factory fodder'. In this respect I did conform to their expectations – I became exactly what they said.

Some teachers were so boring, so indifferent. They would just walk into the class, try and get some order, tell you what page of the book to work from and then sit out the lesson. Some almost seemed to begrudge answering

*questions. One guy always sat there picking his nose and flicking it. You
didn't learn much geography, but by God your reflexes were good!*

After a period of low-paid, unskilled employment and then marriage, many women
awake to a fairly frightening reality and sense of confusion.

*Living on an estate has shown me the feeling of hopelessness that so many
working-class women feel. Trapped by bad education, early marriage and
children. The situation of women who never get together to talk unless it's
about kids or 'the prices'. The feeling that to want something else or more is
odd. I am aware of my ignorance but I have an instinctive feeling about the
injustice of the educational system that turned me loose on the streets at 15
yrs. old knowing all about 1066 and how to make a Christmas cake with the
expectation of working for two or three years. Then marriage. Then kids.
That was success. That was what I had been raised for. Well I have found it
all a con game. It's not enough for me. I need more but I don't know where
to start.*

*I feel very frustrated and sometimes (actually nearly all the time) very angry
at many things happening in our world today, and more so because I don't
feel a part of what is going on. I would like to contribute something in some
way, but I don't know where or how to begin.*

*When I left school I had no qualifications and the types of work open to me
were very limited. There I was – knowing that I wanted to do something,
but lacking the knowledge or the confidence to do anything about it. I felt I
had a lot to give. I wanted to do a worthwhile job. But there were no
openings no-one to show the way. It was really very frustrating. I became
more and more dissatisfied with my own life. I must have been hell to live
with. The dissatisfaction was not a new feeling, I had felt it on and off for
several years but could never actually put a finger on the reason for it – just
the constant thought that there must be more to life than this.*

What Betty Friedan[6] once called the 'problem with no name', the sites and situations different, but the hopelessness of marginality exactly the same. Others recognise
their supposed good fortune – a comfortable home, a decent husband, two lively
children – but still the insignificance and isolation which can, and frequently does,
lead to loneliness, futility and despair.

*I always thought that when people overdose they just calmly fall asleep and
that is the end of that. But I didn't, the aspirins blew the top off my head,
and I was wide awake, fully aware of everything, yet resigned to the fact that
what I'd done, I had wanted to do, because I couldn't find, in all those
years, a way of escaping the misery I felt. I felt guilty at my inability to cope
in situations which only got worse. The frustration of standing at the stove
being totally unable to cook a meal. The lack of concentration when shopping
– grabbing everything just to get away from the place, trembling hands as I
stood in a queue which seemed to have stopped dead. Visiting a friend and as*

*soon as I arrived wanting to leave. Sitting for hours on the bedroom floor
staring into space, not answering the door or phone because I felt so
withdrawn. The effort of making myself drive when I'd lost my confidence.
But in reverse, pacing about like a penned-in tiger feeling I would blow up
any minute if I didn't get out of the house. Floods of tears, feeling helpless
yet frustrated.*

The medical solution? – pills, psychotherapy and hospitalisation. Looked at with
compassion, the idea of medication and behaviour modification intended to adjust
women to the acceptance of unsatisfactory circumstances seems a brutal and insensi-
tive reaction to declarations of inadequacy and despair. But marginality is not a part
of the general experience of men, and remains unnamed as a problem within their
experience. Certainly, if it were, and if men shared on the same scale the futility and
isolation of women's lives, which reduces countless thousands to mental ill health
and dependency on drugs, reactions would be very different. The problem would be
named, it would become a national scandal, a cause for concern and a target for
immediate government action. So long as men do not experience it, however, it is as
though the problem doesn't exist.

The search for understanding and knowledge to deal with feelings of frustration and exclusion has led others up scarcely more illuminating blind alleys – towards
more education, sex and politics.

*I didn't always feel very confident – quite the reverse most of the time, but
because I was reasonably bright (and it was the swinging 60s, remember), I
felt fairly optimistic about my own chances. I had the sense that 'my thing
could happen' – that there must be so much out there – beyond the narrow
confines of that bourgeois, anti-ideas, stultifying atmosphere I grew up in –
that I could reach out to a 'body of knowledge' and make it my own – find
my own oasis and deliverance from feelings of marginality. And so I did
reach out – but 'the knowledge' was all male and the experience wasn't mine
– it was all Sartre, Camus, Colin Wilson, Kerouac, even Nietzche if you
were really into impressing – but I never knew 'til later why I felt wrong –
crazy really, when it all seems so obvious now.*

*The kind of liberation we were being pushed into was sexual liberation. I
remember feeling under great sexual pressure and feeling guilty-prudish – if I
didn't want to screw – like I was suffering from false sexual consciousness
which had to be overcome by correct thinking and practice. And how we
could get abortions pre-67, and afterwards finding a 'friendly' GP who
would give us the pill – he did, but we had to put up with him shoving his
fingers up us, and when we protested, him making obscene comments about
what did we want the pill for, then, if we didn't want to be stuffed? And
having to put up with it because we needed the pill and he was the only one
around who would give it to us. Of course we know now it was all a con,
we were being used yet again. Sexual liberation was merely about removing
even more of the barriers that prevented us being readily available to men.*

When I joined the Campaign Against Racial Discrimination I didn't realise how easy it is to get involved in other people's oppression for the wrong reasons – and it's not to invalidate the process or to deny the anger I felt about it – and still do – but the effect upon one's feelings of marginality – double marginality actually – are enormous. You're 'outside' because you can't concur with the views of mainstream society, and marginal because, by not being black, your role (other than the one prescribed by Stokely Carmichael) is really minimal if you are sensitive to the real issues. It was as if I was so used to feeling for other people, carrying guilt, all those things, that I never stopped to feel for myself. It seems like I've been carrying it all around for a long time now, and whilst my anger about racism has not diminished – my anger about my early blindness to my own position has increased.

Every woman has a well-stocked arsenal of anger, frequently stifled, sometimes turned against herself, but potentially useful against the oppressions, both personal and institutional, which brings that anger into being. In some circumstances it's called guts.

My husband is an alcoholic and after many years of struggle I plucked up courage and got a legal separation. So there I was a single parent living on a council estate, responsible for six kids and of course no maintenance. It took all of this for me to realise how deeply disadvantaged working class families living on low incomes really are. I glibly stated we were hard up – hard up in my mind was temporary – not poor, poor being an attitude of mind in which hope had died and apathy reigned eternal. The school holidays were the worst. We couldn't afford outings or holidays. So I started looking around for some way of compensating. Me and my kids and others who cared to come along walked many miles that first year – to the sports centre, to the common, to the pier – anywhere we didn't have to pay. One day I had fifteen kids with me. About this time Southampton Children's Play Association got off the ground and I became involved, working voluntarily with kids in the school holidays. At first it was very exciting, surely this was the beginning of community action, an activity which the local community would gather round and begin to take stock of their situation and really work to cause some improvement. They would begin to realise that they lived in sub-standard houses, that they had virtually no choice in where they lived or what schools their children were to attend. But none of this happened. I became involved with several other community projects. Always the leaders of these projects were professional people acting out their social consciences in some project that was fashionable at that particular time. Usually up to a point they were successful but always always always they would stick it for a couple of years and when the going got tough they would move onto something more fashionable or lucrative. What all this is leading up to is my feeling of powerlessness that unless I can produce evidence of my success i.e.

commercial, academic or marriage, my opinions will never be considered credible.

Feelings of marginality, powerlessness, isolation and guilt frequently conspire to defuse in women the creative energy of anger.

I remember my lonely anger at issues that arose in my own town, at school, at university where women and girls were so outrageously discriminated against and exploited. The first Abortion Law Reform Act in the late sixties stands out as a monument to the prevailing arrogant attitudes of men who saw themselves as unquestionably able and responsible for debating and legislating on issues that fundamentally were the concern of women. I felt shame and humiliation at that time both personally and on behalf of women everywhere – but guilt too because there was no-one with whom to share these emotions, no-one who could validate me by offering the strength of a similar perception.

Others of us, as women, can seem like agents of our own oppression – until the contradictions become unbearable.

But I, just as much as the males who dominated and legislated for my life's comfort and well-being, was a prisoner of history and culture. To a very large extent I too accepted the **status quo** *as the natural order of things. For all the earlier years of marriage when the children were small, I simply took it for granted that the wife was the home-maker and the husband was the wage-earner, and I took on without question, indeed happily, many of the consequences of this division. There were some things though that I did query but I was made to feel very guilty and ungrateful about these. I felt there was something wrong in the reality that the person who was the wage-earner, was also, almost by that fact, the main decision maker; that the wage earner's time was seen as more valuable, and his opinions better informed and of greater insight than the home-maker's; that his outside commitments, however many hours they occupied, were almost always awarded first priority. These sorts of issues some of them important others less so – that could never be openly talked about because the climate did not allow it, or because they were trivialised, eventually became the focus (still sometimes unspoken) of increasing resentment and recrimination. Much more was added as new attitudes and my own widening experience brought the realisation that these guilt ridden doubts and longings were not after all just the petulant, self-indulgent demands of the discontented child, but the necessary foundations for the wholesome, even though belated, growth of the adult self.*

Growth through anger, focused with precision, can be a powerful source of energy, working towards progress and change. Anger expressed and translated into actions in the service of women's visions and women's futures can be a liberating and strengthening act of clarification, for it is in the painful pursuit of this translation, that we identify who are our genuine allies and who are our enemies.

*For many years he made light of what I did and I endured my frustration in
private. When I became depressed he got heated and said other women were
content why couldn't I be. He said it was my duty to think of the children
and put the family first. I did love the children and they were my salvation in
a way but I found it hard to keep loving him. In fact I felt responsible for
him and guilty – always guilty – but didn't often think in terms of love
anymore. I used to have secret dreams of getting on a plane somewhere –
anywhere – I didn't care – but having the chance to start again. It was all
pipe dreams of course. So long as I put up with it all, and made sure
everyone else was happy, it was alright. When I thought I'd go insane and
started to look outside and find a life for myself he became more obstinate.
He began to trivialise my new interests in education and make sarcastic
remarks about my friends. I suppose he felt jealous and threatened. He
wouldn't look after the children so that I could go out, although he went out
all the time just as he pleased. He even reduced the housekeeping money
because he said I was spending too much of it on myself. When he hit me all
the guilt turned to anger – anger that I had denied my real feelings for so
long, anger that the circumstances in which I lived and which I never
divulged to any other human being nearly cracked me up, and anger that
anyone – especially my husband – could use his physical strength against me
in that way and do what he did. In another way though, it made it easier. I
lost my guilt and any respect I might have had for him. It makes the decision
to get a divorce easier and now there's no turning back.*

For others there are lapses of momentum, because to see clearly the kinds of issues
which women have to confront, needs the strength to renounce the strategies we use
to bind ourselves by our guilt and blind ourselves to the real implications of change.

*I always felt capable of doing something other than translating someone else's
shorthand into legible English but I don't know what. I don't have any
qualifications for anything. I feel very much like the mere appendage of my
family. I'm Paul's wife. Tony and Emma's mother. As my children grow I
become less important to their existence – providing clean clothes and hot
meals – I have to find something more personally fulfilling. I am frustrated
by my inability to do anything well, also worried as I know that whatever
confidence I did possess has been swallowed up somewhere between nappies
and decorating. I want to break out – but feel guilty for wanting something
different. My family seems to constantly expand their lives and I seem to
shrink in amongst them.*

*My own efforts to work out the contradictions and feelings of frustration
within marriage failed. My husband left, but the losses that I felt in
accompaniment with his departure and afterwards were almost overwhelming
– for although I deeply believed in the issues I had been pursuing, I had not
been working from a position of inner strength or personal autonomy. Far
from it. I was in fact still involved in, and even dependent on, some of the*

very supports which in the end had felt like the bars of a restraining cage.
Without them I was lost and frightened, totally self-doubting, hopelessly
uncertain as to which new direction was the one to take.

For many women the feeling of having little confidence is widespread – it represents anxieties which are rarely expressed by men in quite the same way. The feelings are almost always attributed to some sense of personal inadequacy and are strongest when women, used to being home-makers and child-rearers, venture 'out' into the world beyond the home. Many of us underrate our own strengths and achievements, and after a number of years in which our lives have revolved around the needs of our husbands and children, we lose track of our own identity and sense of significance. And yet to collude with this assessment of self-depreciation is to miss several salient points, not least of which is the extent to which self confidence is so often a measure of what is essentially male experience. Women who are educated and qualified, or who do a job that entitles them to wages, or who experience some involvement in public (as distinct from domestic) life – in short, women who are regarded as people in their own right rather than 'merely' someone's wife or someone's mother – are much less likely to feel unconfident than women whose relationships with the outside world are mediated through their relationships with husband and children, and who are defined principally in terms of these relationships. But women, however educationally qualified, career-minded or publicly committed, can automatically withstand the destruction of self-confidence that can accompany domesticity.

> *To suddenly find myself responsible for a child and then a second and a*
> *third, from an area where I had a job I liked and friends, to be out of control*
> *of my own life – only then did I really feel it in my guts that this was it, this*
> *was what it was all about, this is what it is that keeps us in our place.*
> *Children aren't a shared responsibility – they're our responsibility. And*
> *although I knew in my head that it wasn't fair and things should be different*
> *the experience of it all still had the effect of making me feel useless within a*
> *matter of months*

What is being defined as lack of confidence, then, is most frequently the lack of opportunity, the absence from, or the lack of experience of participating in social interaction outside the home which is not predetermined by domestic responsibilities and relationships. In other words, the reality of experiencing a male-centred world as women rather than as men, and blaming ourselves for feeling unconfident about doing those things from which we have been generally excluded.

If the status and significance of the two worlds – public and domestic – were reversed, and the domestic was credited with supreme importance, the majority of men might equally be found lacking in confidence, because their experience would be largely irrelevant and the qualities they had acquired from their socialisation would be seen as less valuable and less appropriate. Women who claim to be unconfident are in most respects internalising and taking responsibility for a process of exclusion and marginalisation which is a consequence of patriarchal relationships. Their acceptance represents a classic example of victimisation and victim blaming rather than the recognition of structural oppression.

Their acceptance is also ironic because the work women undertake at home, the domestic servicing of men and children, the caretaking, and the emotional management of family life at whose centre is the mother, and whose labour and fortitude historically have served to keep families together through often trying and difficult times, represent the kinds of skills and self-sacrifice and resilience which, if they were men's skills and men's work, would be enormously regarded and rewarded.

It seems outrageous that we have allowed any woman who takes on these responsibilities happily, or who endures them with resignation as a fact of life, or who releases herself from them in disenchantment or despair, to feel that she is incapable of anything the. To revalue women's domestic labour and its contribution to the general well-being of others is therefore important – although caring in this way should not be used as a justification for our subordination in society. Women's place is anywhere we want to be in the world, and whilst this might include the home it also, and increasingly, might not. Neither is this to suggest that all women's experience of family life is painful and unhappy. Clearly it is not. Family happiness should not preclude alternative and additional fulfilments – it should enhance them. A woman should not have to choose between the enrichment and development of her own true self and the demands made upon her by her family. But very frequently this is exactly what happens. She denies her own growth in the development of theirs and if, for any reason, things go wrong with those relationships she is left in a more vulnerable position than she would otherwise have been.

The discrepancies between the prevailing view that women should find fulfilment in their families, and the dissatisfactions which confuse, anger and depress so many women, have to be taken seriously. And as increasing numbers of women find themselves, or choose to be, on the outside of conventional two-parent family arrangements, the discrepancy between the myth and reality intensifies. Feelings of marginality, frustration, lack of confidence, personal anonymity and depression are too common among too many women in too many different economic and social circumstances to be dismissed as the disabilities and deficiences of an ungrateful few. Neither is it helpful to have such feelings – different in degree and intensity among different women – diagnosed as hormonal or the emotional consequences of female biology. The root causes are social and are a complement to the subordination of women in a society in which men hold, and have held historically personal and public power. So long as men continue to exercise superordinate control – however gentle, protective, and chivalrous it may seem – women will be encouraged and expected to accept their role in the male scheme of things willingly or dutifully.

Confronted alone, the implications of frustration, anger and change are all too easily doubted and denied, but once women begin to check their experience with each other and begin to name the feelings honestly which get in the way of growth and autonomy, the way is progressively cleared for the creation of very different possibilities. And in this process there is none more competent than another. There are no 'teachers' and no 'learners' – every woman's truth is equally important, as this account makes clear:

> I joined a women's group after the break-up of my marriage which had lasted twenty years. I faced the future with total fear but wanted to feel positive. Early meetings were amazingly different experiences but they shared common features. Firstly was the warmth of acceptance – no passport other than the fact of being a woman was needed – all the usual barriers of age, class, marital status, educational achievement, career or lack of it – were irrelevant. . . We were women and it was understood that there was a shared history and a common experience that could hold us together. From this came a freedom in conversation that was entirely new to me and almost intoxicating in its freshness. Everything was of interest and we were all eager to listen rather than compete for the next cue to offer our own next statement. All the time there was encouragement and validation. I found that so much of my own experience was shared and understood by others. It became clear that so many matters that I had previously felt guilt and shame about were not shameful or morally reprehensible at all – that some of my desires and aspirations were legitimate – and more than that, achievable. I felt strength begin to flow; there was the possibility that the fragmented self could begin to heal and grow again. All the women that I know in the movement are involved in an adventure. We do things which in previous times of our life we would have never thought possible. We dance and make jokes and wear badges that make statements about ourselves that we would never have dared to be let known before. Some women bravely re-start formal education which previously had been halted abruptly in adolescence, others experiment with art or writing or making radio programmes – anything at all, somebody will try. And it is all possible because fundamentally we say 'yes, we know we have potential; we know that each and every one of us has untapped areas of talents that society, or we ourselves, in the condition in which we live, have not been able to fulfil'. We respect each other in whatever we try to do. We don't compete or put down – we combine when that will be fruitful, and give or receive encouragement for whatever we have to do alone. It is early days for me and I have the dilemma of whether, how and when to try and reconcile people from other phases of my life. But what I think is new for me and the others, is that change is happening more rapidly and on many fronts than ever before and we have not just an opportunity but a responsibility, both collectively and personally, to make some statement about it. We may be unsure because for some the opportunity may have been almost forced upon us, and may still be in battle with old attitudes. But I think our responsibility is not to let the wool come down over our eyes again, is to hold to the new awareness that we have gained, and is to stay confident in, and use wherever we can, the strengths that we have gained from our discovery of each other.

Women who join women's groups or who have found with other women understanding and answers that make sense, have not done so out of a general satisfaction with the *status quo*, but from the conscious conviction that as women they are entitled to a fairer, more just and qualitatively richer life. The reconstruction of our world means that the relationships between men and women will have to change if both are not to be dehumanised or destroyed.

In this process of change education both formal and informal has an important part to play. The development of skills to analyse our situation and our condition wisely, the opportunity to learn from the experience of others, and the encouragement to practise our expectation of new possibilities are an essential accompaniment to the material and spiritual independence of women. But the education that will assist women in this quest will also have to be of our own making if it is to take account of our reality and our needs for, as we shall see, that which is, and that which has been provided for us by men is an unreliable ally in the struggle for liberation.

Notes and References

1.   Angela Weaver, 'Prisoners', in *On Second Thoughts*, *(Southampton Women's Education Centre, 1981)*

2.   UK Population 1979: men 27.3 million; women 28.7 million (official government statistics).

3.   Elaine Morgan, *The Descent of Woman*, *(Souvenir Press 1972)*.

4.   Dale Spender, *Man Made Language*, *(Routledge and Kegan Paul, 1983)*

5.   Anna Coote and Beatrix Campbell, *Sweet Freedom,(Picador 1982)*.

6.   Betty Friedan, *The Feminine Mystique*, *(W W Norton 1963)*.

Women and adult education

(Originally published in *Opportunities for Adult Education*,
ed Malcolm Tight, Croom Helm, 1983)

*Throughout the 80s Thompson's pioneering work in Second Chance Education for
women was well established. It moved from its location in the university into the
Women's Education Centre which was founded by Thompson and some of her
students as the first of its kind in the country. The centre was resourced by
Southampton University, the WEA and Hampshire LEA but was organised and
sustained by the collectivity of women who were its members. It survived with its
effective independence intact for ten years, throughout an increasingly inclement
political climate exacerbated by Thatcherism and at a time when cuts were being
made to non-profit making provision and adult education institutions were being
reorganised and restructured. Most of Thompson's theoretical writing in this decade
derived from the inspiration of those she worked with – working class women students
– and from the Women's Education Centre which was her base.*

*In this essay she considers the prevailing state of adult education, using the concept
sexism, which she sees as one of its main operating characteristics. In her examination of the organisation of adult education, of key reports and policy recommendations of the period, and in the core curriculum of local authority and extra mural
provision, she identifies the dilemma whereby men dominated a service which was
effectively dependent upon women and upon men's definitions of what was appropriate for women i.e domestication and leisure frills. Given the wider pecking order
when it comes to what counts as serious and academic knowledge, such provision
could easily be dismissed as inconsequential and unimportant – both in terms of its
clientele and its content. Which was precisely what made it very vulnerable to
government cuts and structural reorganisation. In a sense, the men who had
fashioned and controlled this kind of provision for decades did not, in the end, do
themselves any favours. Neither did they respond positively to the kinds of critique
and the kinds of demand for 'really useful knowledge' that was being made by the
women's movement at the time, except in circumstances in which feminists in adult
education were using the opportunities available at the margins, in a creative – often
subversive – way to advance a different kind of rationale and a different kind of
model in relation to practice. Some of this work – pioneering in the eighties – to do
with access and new opportunities has now become part of the mainstream. But not
always in ways that have retained its critical edge or its anti-sexist stance.*

Women and adult education

Allegations about male sexism and women's oppression in the context of adult education are usually claims which are dismissed as unfounded or tendentious by a profession which considers itself profoundly democratic in its relationships with students, highly responsive to student's needs, and characterised by values and practices which are clearly distinctive when compared with the rest of the education system.

The non-statutory and mainly non-vocational nature of adult education emphasises the voluntary commitment of those who participate. University and Worker's Educational Association (WEA) roots in liberal education assume that students are concerned with the pursuit of knowledge for its own sake rather than for vocational or instrumental purposes, and the local educational authority (LEA) curriculum comprised of practical crafts, physical skills, leisure time and recreational activities, appears to reflect the notion of education for pleasure rather than purpose. Adult education is described as a 'service for the whole community' concerned with 'self fulfilment', 'personal growth and development' and 'useful citizenship'. The rhetoric of its opinion leaders and enthusiasts is unquestioning in commitment, energetic in the pursuit of reform and expansion and critical only of those – either as funding bodies or reluctant recruits – who do not appear to value the significance of what it has to offer.

Theory and practice in adult education reflect a remarkable complacency and consensus. Its philosophy and provision has been infrequently subjected to the kinds of sociological analysis which has become common in the examination of compulsory schooling, so that the links between education and control, education and capitalism and education and culture, for example, have rarely been developed. The early origins of adult education in independent working class movements and sometimes liberal-democratic commitments to the plight of 'the disadvantaged' has meant that the question of social class has been one of academic interest, and there is little evidence of anything other than technical or pathological explanations being given for working class non-participation in adult education[1].

But those who have depicted schooling as a training ground for capitalism[2], and a powerful ideological instrument in the battle for the hearts and minds of dutiful workers[3] have none the less failed to consider the position of women within the education system. The preparation of young women for domesticity and the relationships of reproduction have been generally ignored or treated as subsidiary to the main plot[4]. Only when feminists have entered the debate has discrimination based on gender been taken seriously as a characteristic of all education systems operating within capitalist patriarchy[5]. Indeed, only as a consequence of feminism has the problem of patriarchy – of the power and control which men exercise over women in both private and public relations – been named and exposed as a system of exploitation which is as ubiquitous and as serious in its implications as 'race' and social class[6].

But this analysis applied to education, especially in circumstances in which co-education seems to be reinforcing the underachievement of girls in comparison to boys rather than reducing it[7], has yet to penetrate the general consciousness of adult education theory and practice. Despite a number of obvious contradictions and clear indications of oppression and repression, conventional wisdom within adult education continues to protest its innocence and to deny the patriarchal character and significance of its condition.

Adult education is of course the only sector of the education system in which women as students constitute a significant majority. Women outnumber men in LEA provision by approximately 3 to 1 and in university and WEA provision by approximately 2 to 1. Women are also much more likely than men to make up the groups engaged in non-formal community education, outreach programmes and adult basic education initiatives.

Explanations for women's relatively high participation levels in adult education compared to men, and compared to their lower participation in other forms of post school education provision, are usually couched in terms of social-recreational reasons. The views of a publication by the Northern Advisory Council for Further Education in 1963 concerning women's reasons for attending courses, and offering suggestions to part time teachers of women's subjects, would still go largely unchallenged within contemporary conventional wisdom.

> The desire for the company of others and a change form household duties
> (sic) . . . this recreational attitude and motive is perhaps even more potent in
> the country than the towns for it is in rural districts that the evening class
> provides women with one of the few chances of meeting their friends and
> neighbours[8].

A variation on this theme is the classification of adult education as 'a safe pursuit' which women can go to easily and which provides a female equivalent to the male leisure space of the pub, the golf club or the football game. Given the nature of conventional adult education, it is also seen as an activity which is essentially unthreatening to masculine authority in the home and in the workplace – less threatening, presumably, than if women were to appropriate the pub or the football terraces as their meeting place.

But these explanations are not good enough. They ignore the extent to which the options which women have for cultural and educational expression are seriously restricted compared to men, and more important, the extent to which an essentially female pastime is none the less managed and orchestrated by men within a system of female subordination.

The detailed history of adult education for women in the nineteenth and early twentieth century has still to be written[9] but the indications are that women have always been well represented as students in the mechanics institutes and working men's colleges, the university extension movement and the early WEA, although they were not treated equally with men[10] and the curriculum which they were offered reflected serious problems associated with their subordination to patriarchy. Only in the relatively independent and separatist Co-operative Women's Guilds[11] and in the early women's trade unions did women define and control their own education and seek to further their expectation of an existence which was not bound and restricted by the sexual division of labour in the home and in the demands of capital for a cheap, unskilled, secondary labour force.

The participation of women in the past is of course generally ignored by the historians of adult education, as is the significance of women's majority interest as students in contemporary provision. And seen in this light the career structure of adult education is equally revealing. Women constitute the majority of volunteer tutors in literacy, adult basic education and English as a second language schemes. They are also more likely than men to be part time tutors in local authority provision. As such they have little influence, receive low rates of pay, and enjoy no recognisable career structure except as token women in an essentially male-dominated profession.

Full-time appointments, especially at WEA tutor-organiser and divisional secretary level, university lecturer level and local authority centre principal and advisory level, are predominantly held by men. The fieldworkers and classroom teachers in adult education may well be women but the managers and decision makers, the opinion leaders and rhetoricians, the theorists and philosophers are men – men used to consulting with other men in institutional committees, academic departments, conferences and professional journals. Their assumptions and experience are constructed within a context of male values, male definitions and male authority and are then generalised to represent human assumptions and experience and credited with universal validity and objective truth. Any suggestion that female experience may be different or that women's general exclusion from the power and career structure of adult education seriously distorts the vision and provision of what is offered is rarely conceded by those who monopolise debate. The suggestion made by feminists that male definitions of female need and the patterns of provision that emerge from it are invariably counter-productive in terms of women's *real* needs are all too easily dismissed by men who rarely consult with women on an equal basis and in equal numbers. Most often they ignore the significance of women, thus making us invisible. Just as frequently our significance is assessed in terms of male assumptions about our interests. It's not surprising – given the nature of the society in which we live, in which the sexual division of labour bolsters the economic and the family systems of production – that these are seen as interests restricted to domestic service.

The tendency of the adult education establishment to ignore or to stereotype women in this way is apparent in even the most cursory review of recent literature. In 1973 the Russell Report[12] was welcomed with eagerness and gratitude by fieldworkers at a time when adult education seemed to have lost some of its earlier momentum. The report reminded the service of its origins in working class and independent education and is perhaps best remembered for its encouragement to the WEA particularly to get involved in work with socially and culturally deprived groups, trade union education and political education. Given the close association of adult education in its formative years with social and political movements seeking social change, and given the loyal participation of women in the university extension movement and the WEA, it is perhaps surprising to find the Russell committee making precious little reference to women and no reference whatsoever to one of the most significant, voluntary, independent, political, educational and spontaneous grass roots movements of recent times – the women's movement.

The re-emergence of feminism in Britain in and around 1968 was accompanied by a proliferation of informal meetings, study groups, conferences, newsletters and publications which, although related to campaigns and the concern to change the subordinate position of women in society, also reflected a serious educational purpose and commitment. Feminists within adult education have seen to it that adult education classes increasingly reflect the interests and concerns of this important popular movement, but five years after its appearance, in the wake of similar developments in Europe and North America, and amidst considerable publicity and public discussion, the Russell committee, defending more than a century of popular and political education, was apparently oblivious to its significance.

Women are rarely mentioned in the report except to register that they constitute a majority of students, but when they are, it's as mothers – even working mothers – rather than women that they are defined. A single sentence of the report calls for attention to the needs of women in industry, but whilst this is seen as important 'for their own intellectual progress', more significance is attached to 'their influence on their children'.

> The working mother is particularly important, perhaps with a special
> educational need, and as many more women will be at work in the coming
> decades, the influence of working mothers on children at the starting point of
> the whole learning process will spread widely. There will be a need for adult
> education to ensure that this is a supportive influence.

It is noticeable that 'working fathers' are not charged with the same responsibilities for the pre-school education of their children and that women as political activists, trade unionists, seekers after truth, feminists, full-time workers and major breadwinners in single parent households, among many other possibilities, are still subsumed within the primary concept 'mother'. So far as Russell was concerned women were only visible as mothers and totally invisible in every other respect.

In 1978 Graham Mee and Harold Wiltshire produced a report on local authority adult education entitled *Structure and Performance*[13]. Their investigation made it clear that, despite claims to the contrary about 'meeting individual needs' and 'responsiveness to local communities and conditions', an amazing consensus exists throughout LEA non vocational adult education about what kinds of provision ought to be offered. Wiltshire and Mee do not utilise the classification 'women's interests' which appears in countless institute prospectuses and centre programmes, preferring 'crafts and arts', 'physical activities', 'cognitive skills' and the like. If they had, their findings may have been even more revealing and disturbing for the core curriculum in local authority adult education is little more than an inventory of traditional female skills concerned primarily with domestic management (e.g. hostess cookery, creative embroidery, flower arranging, soft furnishing and machine knitting); personal relationships (e.g. child development, encounter groups and co-counselling); and physical appearance (e.g. make-up and beauty care, home hairdressing and ladies keep fit). Wiltshire and Mee hesitate to explain and indeed claim, 'not to know what the processes are that determine and maintain this consensus and what the channels are through which they operate'. For feminists they are obvious. The common denominator of course is the definitions of relevance and the assumptions held about students which those responsible for provision reproduce with monotonous regularity and tenacious predictability every year in every corner of the country.

They operate according to a series of social imperatives which conform women to close allegiance with their traditional roles. They service the 'vocation' of homemaker, wife and mother and despite declarations about student *self*-fulfilment and *personal* development they exist primarily to reinforce the obligations women are usually assigned to enhance the care and comfort of others.

In 1979 the Advisory Council for Adult and Continuing Education produced a Strategy for the Basic Education of Adults[14]. The report committee was chaired by Henry Arthur Jones – already a considerable influence in Adult Education circles on the subject of 'disadvantage'. The report has been quite properly criticised for its failure to examine the structural causes of economic and social disadvantage and its presentation of adults who are assumed to be in need of basic education as in some way responsible for their own ineptitude[15]. The analysis is of course consistent with Jones's earlier contributions to the Russell report and with Peter Clyne's research [16], and with the proliferation of social policy statements concerned to keep public spending to a minimum and to blame the victims of social inequality and oppression rather than the social and economic arrangements which capitalism promotes to further the interests of dominant groups.

But the report is also disturbing in its implications for women. As usual the fact that women constitute a large proportion of the participants engaged in adult basic education schemes is ignored and women are subsumed within the general categories 'parents', 'adults', 'immigrants' and 'students'. And yet the language and tone of the report, couched in terms of caring and confidence and coping, reflect implicit assumptions about women which need to be examined carefully. The language is certainly not of the variety which would be applied to male industrial workers, students on vocational courses or those engaged in prestigious academic study. And seen in this light the report is very worrying. The 'feminine' nature of the language and the assumptions which it records are not to women's advantage because they rely on constructions of female need in circumstances in which men are the 'authority', the providers and the need meeters, and women are the functionaries and the recipients. The stereotypes which emerge are of feckless, pathetic, unconfident individuals in need of remedial education and behaviour modification, encoded in the kinds of coping and caring courses offered to less able and less amenable pupils in schools.

The life skills prescribed specifically for women are those which assist in domestic management and health and family relations – a confirmation of women's traditional roles with an insinuation that professional intervention is necessary to ensure that they are performed satisfactorily.

If women really are disadvantaged because of limited opportunities, or poverty, or their social class position, or their ethnic status in a racist society, or their subordination to men, learning to cope – to put up with – unsatisfactory circumstances, defined as an essential life skill, can hardly be described, as the report claims, to be concerned with the pursuit of personal development and self confidence.

So long as the opinion leaders and policy makers in adult education continue to describe the world as though women don't exist, or to associate women simply with domesticity and child rearing, adult education will continue to reinforce inequality between the sexes to the long term detriment of both men and women. In the short term, the sexist condition of adult education produces a number of interesting contradictions. We have seen how adult education is presented as a resource for the whole community and is concerned with general educational aims like personal growth and development, responsible citizenship and the creation of self confidence. And yet the core curriculum of local authority provision is rooted in domestic management, recreational activities and relationship skills. As Nell Keddie[17] points out, adult education has made women's work its curriculum and represented it to women as skills in which they are deficient and yet, at the same time, is embarrassed to promote itself as a profession which services domestic labour. The dilemma of the opinion leaders and theoreticians becomes increasingly difficult in the face of criticisms about indulging petit bourgeois consumerism and wasting public money on fripperies and leisure frills.

> The public rhetoric of adult education claims that it is a universalistic service which provides for the whole community and we can see that attacks on cake icing and flower arranging threaten to expose the limitations of this claim. To confront it adequately would expose not only that women are the main users of adult education but that the LEA curriculum is strongly located in the home and in women's activities[18].

Keddie points out that this dilemma is not made explicit but means that adult education has to justify what is generally regarded as trivial and frivolous whilst, on the other hand, taking care to disguise the extent to which its professional status depends upon servicing women's work. Keddie's contribution[19] to our understanding of the limitations imposed upon the curriculum of local authority provision because of sexist assumptions is invaluable although rarely conceded by those responsible for organising provision. The suggestion that the core curriculum of university and WEA provision is also sexist, albeit in a different way, is also denied.

The liberal tradition associated with this provision has progressively abandoned any early commitment it might have had to 'really useful knowledge'[20] concerned with social change. Its roots in academic scholarship and the patronage of the leisured and genteel classes in the nineteenth century[21] has contributed to the sense of detachment from contemporary society. Current defenders of this legacy still advocate it in preference to the 'practical instrumentalism' which they associate with more recent developments like trade union studies and community education, preferring adult education's 'traditional role of general cultural diffusion and personal development through studies on a broad perspective'[22]. The extent to which 'general cultural diffusion' actually means 'dominant cultural diffusion' has been well argued by those commentators critical of the cultural exclusivity of so much university and WEA provision. But it is important to realise that this knowledge – seemingly 'the best that has been thought and said', the renowned and universally accredited epitome of our cultural and academic heritage – is, in fact, a form and variety of knowledge selected, constructed, protected and disseminated within the historical context of male supremacy.

Considerable scholarship by feminists on both sides of the Atlantic has revealed the extent to which the male academic tradition and the knowledge which it has created is only a partial definition of reality, which has consistently discounted female experience and erased it from the records.[23] The criticism made by Otto Rank in 1958[24] about psychology 'that it is not only man made . . . but masculine in its mentality' has increasingly been applied to all other disciplines including the so called neutral sciences. The significance of the increasing demand for Women's Studies courses in adult and higher Education is a recognition of the extent to which conventional academic scholarship and the curriculum which it provides is viewed by feminists as a system celebrating predominantly male knowledge, values and achievements[25].

Seen in this context it is not just that women are channelled into certain kinds of 'female' subject areas but that within certain subject areas women do not appear to feature at all. the study of history, philosophy, religion, art, music and the like is very much a consideration of male interests and achievements. The social conditions which produced such achievements and have accorded them so much value and prestige are left unquestioned. Through this kind of educational transmission in extramural and WEA classes both men and women subscribe to the belief in female inferiority and male supremacy. Nor is it simply a question of reducing a bias which has largely ignored women's experience and exploits. Women have been, and continue to be, left out of the discourses which construct the knowledge that is considered valuable in the first place.

Dorothy Smith[26] puts it like this:

Women have been largely excluded from producing the forms of thought and the images and symbols in which thought is expressed and ordered. There is a circle effect. Men attend to and treat as significant what men say. The circle of men whose writing and talk was significant to each other extends backwards in time as far as our records reach. What men were doing was relevant to men, was written by men about men for men. This is how a tradition is formed.

The contradiction of this kind of adult education, so far as women are concerned, is that an essentially female student body is engaged in a form of learning, and in the pursuit of knowledge controlled by men, which takes very little account of the social, political, economic and cultural conditions of being female and which, in the guise of liberal studies, operates to confirm illiberal discrimination against women.

A further contradiction lies in the problems and possibilities associated with marginality. Adult education is the poorest and meanest outpost of the education system – a service which Mike Newman has referred to as 'the poor cousin'[27]. In terms of the educational pecking order in further and higher education, adult education enjoys the least prestige. This is one reason presumably why women have been allowed to monopolise its provision. And because women have monopolised its provision and been offered, in educational terms, fairly low status knowledge, it has been difficult to argue the case for more prestige or more resources. The incidence of women's participation is at the same time ignored and yet held to be responsible for adult education's weak position. Current arguments about adult education as 'the cure' for unemployment, and discussions about paid educational leave, continuing education and retraining are invariably debated in the context of male industrial workers and manpower requirements[28]. If, as the ACACE report, *Continuing Education – From Policies to Practice*[29] recommends, all adults should be entitled to continuing opportunities for education throughout their lives and the education of adults should be given increasing priority in the allocation of resources, the odds against either women as a group or mainstream adult education monopolised by women benefitting from such developments are tremendous. It is no coincidence that the expansion in training and retraining which has taken place has done so under the auspices of the Manpower Services Commission and the further education sector; and that discussions within the universities, for example, about mature students and the opportunities offered to universities by promoting continuing education programmes have been taken over by internal departments looking to consolidate their positions in periods of retrenchment, rather than departments of extra mural studies whose low esteem and weakness in the intellectual and political pecking order is only too apparent.

And yet for feminists, the relative accessibility of adult education and its potentially sympathetic rhetoric about 'student centredness' and 'student responsiveness' and, in the WEA at least, its proclaimed commitment to student democracy and accountability, all represent possibilities in which the preponderance of women could be seen as a strength rather than a weakness. If nothing else it provides the opportunity for women to meet, to generate their own knowledge and to become their own teachers. Certainly Women's Studies courses organised in the context of adult education are proving to be an important connecting point between informal expression of feminist demands and dissatisfactions and the translation of these into political and cultural practices which consolidate the growing rejection of patriarchal authority by increasing numbers of women.

In Southampton, for example, the Women's Studies programme has grown from modest beginnings in neighbourhood action groups, trade union meetings and women's liberation concerns into a thriving programme which not only provides an alternative curriculum to that which is consistent with patriarchal provision but which engages a wide cross section of women in the exploration of feminism. Strong roots in Second Chance Education, which positively discriminates in favour of working class women who have received least from the education system in the past, have ensured that new developments have remained committed to the needs of all women rather than the concerns of those who more easily monopolise provision. But the energy and preoccupations of feminist women have also been an important catalyst in the elaboration and development of this work. In 1981 we were able to open the country's first Women's Education Centre in which the shared resources of the university, the LEA and the WEA are combined to provide a comprehensive range of courses and activities which take serious account of women's concerns as they are defined by women themselves. The Centre is responsible to the women who are its members and decisions about Centre policies and activities are taken collectively. Funding from the Equal Opportunities Commission has provided a measure of independence and there is a growing sense of control being exercised directly by the participants of the Centre rather than by external funding bodies.

In other areas Women's Studies programmes, women's trade union studies, New Opportunities for Women courses, re-entry to education and employment projects and a whole range of short courses, day schools and conferences related to campaigns concerned with, for example, child care, male violence, equal opportunities at work, health issues and the women's peace movement have all provided educational support to women who do not want to be confined by their traditional and domestic roles. And all of these have been argued for and established within the parameters of conventional provision. They are the developments which the men who monopolise decision-making power in adult education must be persuaded to take more seriously.

But encouraging women's access to institutions created and controlled by men, or demanding that the reality of adult education increasingly lives up to the rhetoric, is only half the battle. So long as men continue to control the organisation and provision of adult education, and so long as male-centred knowledge and relevance defined in male terms continues to determine the nature of the curriculum, then women's experience and expectations will continue to be discounted. If male power holders in adult education are genuinely concerned to promote equality of opportunity between the sexes, and to provide the space for women to create and control their own education free from the impositions of vested male interests, then they must equally be prepared to let women get on with it themselves and be prepared to relinquish the authority, and power and influence which their control implies. In the education system generally men control 97 per cent of the government of education [30]. The distribution in adult education is nor radically different. Only when this is shared on a fifty-fifty basis with women, and when the cultural heritage and validity of women's experience is reflected in the curriculum, shall we begin to imagine an education system which serves both sexes equally.

Notes and References

1. See Jane Thompson (ed), *Adult Education for a Change* (Hutchinson, 1980)
2. See, for example, Samuel Bowles and Herb Gintis, *Schooling in Capitalist America* (Routledge and Kegan Paul, 1976); Dale, Esland and Macdonald (eds), *Schooling and*

Capitalism: A Sociological Reader (Routledge and Kegan Paul 1976); Geoff Whitty and MFD Young (eds), *Society, State and Schooling* (Falmer Press 1977).

3. Louis Althusser, 'Ideology and Ideological State Apparatuses – Notes Towards an Investigation', *Lenin and Other Essays* (New Left Books 1971).

4. Note, for example, Paul Willis's almost total lack of reference to the cultural, social and educational experience of girls in *Learning to Labour – How Working Class Kids Get Working Class Jobs* (Saxon House, 1979).

5. See, for example, Dale Spender and Elizabeth Sarah (eds), *Learning to Lose* (The Womens Press, 1980); Dale Spender *Invisible Women – The Schooling Scandal* (Writers and Readers Co-operative, 1982); Rosemary Deem *Women and Schooling* (Routledge and Kegan Paul, 1978).

6. See, for example, Jane Thompson, *Learning Liberation: Women's Response to Men's Education* (Croom Helm 1983).

7. See Spender *Invisible Women* op cit.

8. *Suggestions for Part Time Teachers of Women's Subjects*, 4th Edition (Northern Advisory Council for Education, 1963).

9. But see June Purvis, 'Working Class Women and Adult Education in Nineteenth Century Britain', *History of Education* Vol 9 no 3 (Taylor and Francis, 1980).

10. In the institutes and colleges, for example, women did not pay the same dues as men and were excluded from voting rights on matters concerning institute policy and curriculum.

11. Margaret Llewelyn Davies (ed), *Life As We Have Known It, by Cooperative Working Women* (Virago, 1977)

12. The Russell Report *Adult Education: A Plan for Development* (HMSO 1973).

13. Harold Wiltshire and Graham Mee, *Structure and Performance in Adult Education* (Longman, 1978).

14. *A Strategy for the Basic Education of Adults* (ACACE, 1979).

15. By Nell Keddie and Jane Thompson, for example, in *Adult Education for a Change*.

16. Jone's and Clyne's cooperation on a research project based at the University of Leicester became incorporated into the policy proposals of Russell and is elaborated in Clyne's book, *The Disadvantaged Adult* (Longman 1972).

17. Nell Keddie, unpublished paper, forthcoming.

18. ibid.

19. ibid.

20. See Richard Johnson, 'Really Useful Knowledge, Radical Education and Working Class Culture' in Clarke, Critcher and Johnson (eds), *Working Class Culture* (Hutchinson 1979).

21. Raymond Williams in *The Long Revolution* (Penguin, 1961) distinguishes four sets of educational philosophies or ideologies which rationalise different emphases in the selection of the content of the curricula, and relates these to the social position of those who hold them. The liberal position he associates with the nineteenth century aristocracy and gentry.

22. KH Lawson, 'Community Education: A Critical Assessment' *Adult Education* vol 50 no 1 (NIACE 1977).

23. See, for example, Dale Spender (ed), *Men's Studies Modified* (Pergammon Press, 1981) and Adrienne Rich, *On Lies Secrets and Silences* (Virago, 1980).

24. Otto Rank, *Beyond Psychology* (Dover, 1958).

25. Thompson, *Learning Liberation*, op cit.

26. Dorothy Smith, 'A Peculiar Eclipsing, Women's Exclusion from Men's Culture', *Women's Studies International Quarterly*, Vol 1 no 4 (Pergammon Press 1978).

27. Mike Newman, *The Poor Cousin: A Study of Adult Education* (Allen and Unwin, 1979).

28. Thompson *Learning Liberation* op cit.
29. *Continuing Education; From Policies to Practice* (ACACE 1982).
30. Eileen Byrne, *Women and Education* (Tavistock, 1978).

The cost and value of higher education to working class women

(Originally published in *Oxford and Working Class Education:
A New Introduction to the 1908 Report,* ed Sylvia Harrop,
Continuing Education Press, University of Nottingham, 1987)

*In this essay Thompson uses the opportunity of re-introducing the 1908 Report to
reflect on the position of working class women in higher education. She comments on
the extent to which the condition 'working class' has evolved as a male construct,
which seriously underestimates the extent to which working class women are 'the true
radicals' and which does not give credit to the support networks which exist between
working class women in the pursuit of survival as being anything to do with a political
movement – which she argues they are.*

*In the eigthies it was still rare for working class women to become mature students in
higher education, despite the increasing respectability of access courses and the
introduction of Government directives to open up higher education to more non
tradtional students. It still is. Although higher education would now be viewed as a
much less elitist affair – at least in the new universities and former polytechnics – the
financial constraints around grants, a punitive Benefit System, the collapse of
pastoral and personal tutor systems as student numbers increase, the fragmentation
of knowledge into modular degrees and the re-invention of a two-tier system to
protect elite and patriarchal interests all preclude much participation in practice by
working class women.*

*Writing in the grip of Thatcherism – with its particularly harsh effects on the lives of
poor people, including working class women, Thompson is merciless about the quasi-
liberal optimism that is frequently invested in the prevailing education system as a
source of liberation for working class women.*

The cost and value of higher education to working class women

There is not much of significance in the 1908 Report for working class women. A lot of mention is given to the concerns of men and, whilst we may choose to interpret the reference to 'work people' as also including women, there is little evidence that the political, economic and social concerns of women were given much consideration by those who produced the report. Not that many women – let alone working class women – could expect to become university students in 1908. The campaigns of the early feminists had gone some way to opening up the universities and some of the professions to middle class women but the conditions placed upon their participation and survival were enormous; and although some Oxford colleges were taking women undergraduates in 1908, they were not giving them degrees until 1927.

The demand for education from working class women was – as it is now – even more difficult. In the day-to-day struggle for economic survival – set in the context of arduous and interminable physical labour – the opportunities for educational pursuits were limited. In the nineteenth century most of what was provided 'officially' in mechanics institutes and working men's colleges – which, despite their male identi-fied names did provide classes for women – was heavily influenced by restricted views of women's 'natural' predilection for domestic labour. It was only really in separatist organisations like the Women's Cooperative Guilds, The Suffrage Movement and the early women's trade unions that women's own definitions of 'really useful knowledge'[1] were allowed to surface. In these organisations working class women became skilled in political organising and campaigning and constructed educational programmes for themselves which did justice to the realities of the social and economic conditions in which they lived. It's interesting to remember that in all of these organisations working class women met major opposition from their fellow men, who did not respond at all well to women taking political action on their own or, more importantly, stepping outside their traditional and allotted roles. And whilst women made up a considerable proportion of the emergent Workers Educational Association (WEA), passing the kinds of resolutions about child care provision at courses, women-only classes and relevant curriculum which sound all too familiar today, the official historical voice of the movement has remained obsessively male.

It always strikes me that if an alien from another planet was ever motivated to research and understand the political, social and cultural history of the working class in Britain, this one fact before all others would be obvious. It is an account of a tradition, of a condition, of a vision, which is almost exclusively male. It's a fact which escapes alomost everyone else, however. The working class are written about and talk about themselves (those who are asked) as if women don't exist. Or as if the issues and experiences which characterise women's lives can be subsumed neatly within the general categories applied to the class as a whole. The notion is that what is good for or bad for the working class is experienced similarly by both sexes. But when looked at from the standpoint of women this is clearly not the case. For example, working class women could justifiably object to the united efforts of employers and trade unionists historically to downgrade and de-skill women's work and to reinforce women's economic dependency on men by the creation of the 'family wage' and its payment to male breadwinners. And so long as the responsibility for clild care, for example, is not seen as a central and fundamental issue in discussions to do with the distribution of paid work and wages, then the very real restrictions imposed on women as workers are not being taken seriously, or even into account, in some of the major economic decisions of the day. Working-class men – just as much as their middle class masters – benefit enormously from women's unpaid domestic labour at home and however strong their resistance to the bosses might be, their resistance rarely extends to hatred of the bosses' system which operates on the basis of patriarchy, just as surely as it does on capitalism and racism.

The re-examination of the concept working class, viewed from the perspective of women's experiences, is not the major concern of this chapter however – except to draw readers' attention to the ease with which women's experiences get subsumed within male experience to the extent that they become invisible.[2] This tendency, rooted in patriarchal power as a world view, is arguably just as common today as it was in 1908. A similar group of working class and liberal men meeting to debate some contemporary issue in adult education would do so in much the same vein as their fathers did before them. Except, of course, that now there would be less excuse for their ignorance.

The writers of the 1908 Report were preoccupied with two concerns – that working men should have access to the excellence of Oxford and that Oxford should have access to the hearts and minds of working men. Neither side envisaged the radical transformation of education or society as a consequence, although they were intent upon achieving some modification and shift in the social class divide.

Those who contributed to the writing of the Oxford Report were principally concerned that the alleged excellence of university education should be more widely available and that the rarified and privileged colleges of Oxbridge should be opened up – democratised and reconstituted – to make room for the working class. Education should concentrate on politically and socially useful knowledge and those chosen and enabled to study should be encouraged to return to the service of their class as trade union officials, labour representatives and teachers.

In practice, except for a few notable exceptions, the older universities, especially Oxford and Cambridge, have remained as training grounds for the rich and influential. Possibly the numbers of Labour MPs who have been educated there has increased over the years – but this is more a reflection of changes in the class composition of the Labour Party than the penetration of elite institutions by working class students. And so far as working class women are concerned, the numbers entering any form of higher education has remained consistently insignificant. It's not really surprising when you think about it. Universities were founded for the sons of white upper and middle class men to help reproduce and consolidate their influence and power. Women were admitted reluctantly at the end of the nineteenth century and still constitute a major minority of the students in scientific and technical subjects and of the post-graduates in all subjects. The control, administration and teaching in our universities, polytechnics and colleges of higher education is still a predominantly male preserve. Women are enormously outnumbered at every level of teaching and policy making in higher education and our influence, has been minimal in terms of challenging or transforming the definitions of knowledge and learning which these institutions reflect.

Women who enter higher education do so principally to learn more about men – about male ideas – and about male ways of doing things. It's not usual to classify higher education as men's education although the description is a useful one.[3] Centuries of philosophy and selection have gone into the creation of what counts as important knowledge. Notions of reason and logic and objectivity have been constructed to obscure the extent to which what emerges is a reflection of male experience and male priorities. It is unlikely to be otherwise so long as women's experiences of the world – our ideas and achievements and struggles, our priorities and allegiances – remain largely unrecorded by the men who have had the power historically to decide what is considered important.

Although studies in the sociology of knowledge have come to similar conclusions about the effects of social class and 'race' on the construction and transmission of what constitutes knowledge, less attention has been paid except by feminists – to the influences of patriarchal authority in the process of defining ideas and recording experience. So far as feminist thinkers are concerned, that which counts as education reflects a partial though powerful view of reality: a view which pays little or no attention to the historical, political and cultural concerns of women or which makes reference to women only in the context of a range of ideologies based on notions of male supremacy.[4]

When the authors of the 1908 Report attributed great significance to the quality of education available at Oxford, it was a masculine excellence which they were talking about. But then it was also men whom they imagined would be the recipients. And if they were unaware of sexual bias, they were more conscious that elitism and class privilege could cause the kinds of prejudice and assumptions in teachers and fellow students which would be unconducive to the participation of working class people. The solution to this problem was seen in terms of securing some kind of control over who would be allowed to teach and some consultation about what curriculum would be considered relevant. They were wise to be suspicious. Exactly the same reservations should be expressed today in relation to women's education. Access to institutions of higher education, in which the majority of teachers are men, in which the curriculum is an historic reflection of men's ideas and concerns and in which the values, attitudes and assumptions which predominate are patriarchal, is a poor consolation for women.

The Report writers were naive to imagine that they could exercise some control over all this on behalf of working class students, however. Those who are dominant in our culture are unlikely to concede their predominance to others whose political interests are not consistent with their own. The control and dissemination of ideas, and the selection of those who will be given access to them, is a major political strategy in the preservation of power by the ruling class. It is unlikely to be given up easily. Those from the working class who have been allowed to learn these lessons have done so as individuals not as a class – and with the intention of enlisting them as allies or 'responsible citizens' – which is probably the same thing.

The Report writers were also naive to put so much faith in the 'good intention' of education and educationalists. Education is not a neutral or a dispassionate pursuit of truth or excellence. It is part of the logic and order of the prevailing system, a system which is not renowned for its commitment to the transformation of class society. A limited transfusion of brains and energy from working class sources has the double attraction to the ruling class of co-opting possible adversaries and utilising their abilities and of demonstrating an openness and accessibility to opportunity which makes it seem that working class inequality is not the social institution which socialists and other critics suppose it to be. In practice, of course, there has been no major redistribution of power in the control and management of education and ideas since the 1908 Report was written. The means of communication and shift in emphasis towards popular and mass media may well have changed the style and the presentation of the message over the years, but those in control of the dominant culture come from much the same political and social groups, with the same interests to defend, as they always did.

Women should learn from this experience. Access to institutions on an individual basis to satisfy individual ambitions is unlikely either to transform those institutions' perceptions of themselves and the values they promote, or to encourage changes that will contribute to the political advantage of women generally. Women should be wary of attributing liberationary intentions to an education system based on both class and patriarchal privileges. It is a common misconception that education is an enlightening endeavour which can change attitudes and encourage reform – especially in matters to do with sexual prejudice and discrimination.[5] Rather, the education system is the creation of sexual prejudice and discrimination, which so long as it continues to reflect male concerns, and is kept under the control of men,[6] will remain an unlikely ally in the pursuit of women's liberation.[7]

To suggest that working-class people cannot use the skills of learning, thinking and argument to assist them in their resistance to class oppression and in the pursuit of social change is clearly untrue, however. The capacity to analyse and conceptualise clearly and to generate knowledge which is useful in a political and social sense are two of the traditional concerns of working class radicals. Perhaps we should not judge the authors of the 1908 Report too harshly for their misplaced trust in the good faith of the universities like Oxford to respond to their demands, except that others of their contemporaries were more astute in their assessment of class allegiance and put their energies·elsewhere.[8]

So far as working class women are concerned, the opportunities to participate in adult and higher education have not changed significantly since 1908. Much of what is currently provided in local authority provision, community education and adult basic education, continues with the same oppressive assumptions about women's limitations and deficiencies that have always characterised the mass education of working class women[9], whilst participation in higher education, for the most part, implies enormous personal costs which are rarely publicised or acknowledged by the institutions involved.

The mid-1980s are not a hopeful or inspiring time for women generally – especially working class women. For a brief period in the late sixties and early seventies, when the economy was expanding, the numbers of women entering the workforce and the trade union movement increased. Progressive ideas in education attributed great significance to the spread of comprehensive education and co-education in schools and to the expansion and democratisation of higher education. The United Nations Decade for Women began in Britain with the passing of Equal Pay and Anti-Sex Discrimination legislation and generally more enlightened attitudes about women's rights became the proclaimed concern of every self-respecting liberal. Although Women's Liberation provided a rich resource for trivialisation by the media, there was a sense in which, if women's demands were not too extreme, and were easily satisfied by a few minor modifications in the administration of sexual discrimination, then the liberal-socialist establishment would be happy to make the appropriate gestures.

Ten years later, however, the picture is very different. Women are back in the trenches under siege. The expansion of women's jobs in the welfare and service industries has been severely cut back by successive governments' economic policies. Part-time women workers have been laid off more quickly and more assiduously than any other group of workers – most of them with no recourse to unemployment benefit. The services which once assisted families in the care of children and dependent relatives – services which women in the seventies were paid to provide – have now largely disappeared, leaving unpaid women at home with the main responsibility for 'community care'. For working class families particularly, the economic depression of the eighties has returned enormous numbers of people to the poverty and insecurity of the thirties. Today increasing numbers of women face the consequences of this on their own as the state-dependent leaders of single parent families. Whatever anger or outrage the all-but-defeated labour movement can generate on behalf of the unemployed and on the loss and destruction of their jobs is reserved for men and young people. The popular image of unemployment is one of men wasting their time at home or rioting on the streets and football terraces. The socialist view is of men stripped of their dignity and robbed of their inheritance. The extent of women's poverty and response to unemployment remains an enigma hidden behind the home front, where lack of money, lack of power and lack of hope accentuate the struggles which have always occurred there between unequals. The law calls them 'domestic disputes' and is reluctant to get involved. Women call them bullying and intimidation, GBH, sexual abuse and murder. In other circumstances – on the streets or the football terraces for example – they would be called civil war.

The legacy of the enlightenment of the seventies means that it is still politically unacceptable for governments, employers and trade unions to say explicitly that women should stay at home and give their jobs to men, but there is little question that the increase in unemployment has been paralleled by an intensification of family-centred propaganda which seeks to hold women personally responsible for the mental and social health of men and children unsettled by insecurity, poverty and lack of prospects – as well as urging the retreat from feminist ideas about autonomy and equality.

The majority of working class women, because of the association of feminism with middle class behaviour and impossible dreams, are unlikely to call themselves feminists in fact. But this doesn't mean that they are complacent about the injustices of life. Beatrix Campbell[10] argues very convincingly that it is working class women, rather than men, who are the true radicals – despite the adulation which is usually reserved by the Left for working class heroes. And although powerless in most respects and dependent on men or the state economically, it would be wrong to see working class women simply as the victims of oppression. Rather they are the survivors, the ones whose resilience historically has kept families and communities together – women who have gritted their teeth and endured and picked their way courageously through the blood and guts and mess that men leave behind. Most working class women both accept and resent the power of men in their lives. Their presence seems inevitable – at times it brings happiness – often it's just the way things are. But women also know, what their mothers and sisters have always understood, that it is not men but other women – family, friends and workmates – who provide the life-sustaining relationships which keep us all going. I have yet to see any serious validation given to the support which women give to each other in working class communities which recognises it as a political affiliation – a movement. It is more common to associate what counts as politics with the labour movement – a movement which men have created and within which men meet to decide priorities and strategies. Sited in the Labour Party, the trade unions and the working men's clubs, the participation of women has always been peripheral and subsidiary – though not for the want of trying. This – what Beatrix Campbell calls the 'men's movement' – which earlier radicals might well have looked to for inspiration and leadership in the defence of working class interests – is currently in disarray. The incoherence of the left, the divisions between different groups and tendencies and the ever-increasing slide towards the politics of appeasement and the middle ground, has left a void which accentuates the hopelessness of contemporary class struggle. Working class women might do better to put their faith in feminism – albeit a feminism rooted in working class experience and realities – which would at least begin with some understanding of the ways in which class, 'race' and gender inequalities intersect to the multiple detriment of women, and which could identify priorities from the standpoint of women which usually go unnoticed or ill-considered by those who most often speak for the working class.

It is precisely this starting point – the interplay between class and gender oppression – which has informed the women's education programme in Southampton for the last seven or eight years. It is not a programme which is particularly well received by the university[11] nor is it principally concerned with the preparation of working class students for higher education. But over the years a goodly number of working class women, with minimum schooling and no formal qualifications, have chosen to go on to higher education once their course with us is completed.

It would be wrong of me to suggest that this choice is misconceived. With the fewest of options available to working class women generally, and with only limited choices in terms of occupation and lifestyle, anything which helps to widen those limitations must be welcomed. Although qualifications do not provide an automatic route to economic independence they can, in some circumstances, make a difference. I have known women for whom the experience of higher education has been a good one – who have flourished intellectually and who have claimed the right, still so frequently monopolised by another class and another sex, to be academics – women who, on behalf of others, have established their right of entry – as proper students – into institutions which other women of their class are usually only allowed to cook for or clean. I suppose there is a long established argument in socialist politics – which also influenced the writers of the 1908 Report which is that working class people have just as much right to enjoy 'the best' as anyone else. If I sound sceptical about all of this, it is because I have yet to be convinced that what higher education represents is the best, or that the price which working class women pay to have a taste of it is worth the cost.

I suppose I am more pleased to report that the radical expectation that workers will not merely use higher education for personal advancement, but as a way of gaining useful knowledge and skills which they can then use to work with, and on behalf of, other members of their class, has been a common commitment among women I have known. Two of the teachers on our current Second Chance for Women programme, for example, were originally students on the same scheme and a fair number of others have returned after graduation, to work in legal and advice centres, in community and social work and in women's projects of various kinds. For those whose commitment to class rather than loyalty to the state is strong, the workplace is often a keen site of struggle. But it is not higher education that has made the difference – it is their politics and their allegiance which is the crucial connection. For every woman who has flourished in the company of middle class ideas and values and at the hands of predominantly middle class men, however, there have been many others – the majority I would say – who have had at best a mixed experience and at worst a very distressing time.

Most obviously there are the problems to do with the curriculum of higher education: the reality, as a working class woman, of feeling totally submerged in a sea of attitudes, ideas, factual information and assumptions, built around a middle class male view of the world which has changed only slightly, it would seem, since I was at university myself 20 years ago. When I look at the eight long rows of books in my study, gathering dust now because I don't read them any more, which are the legacy of my university days and early teaching career, books which represent the significant arguments and ideas in education, history, sociology, politics and literary criticism, I can find only two – one by Simone de Beauvoir and one by Virginia Woolf – written by women. The same books in virtually the same proportions still appear on the reading lists my current ex-students show me. It is not only the official curriculum, though, but also the hidden curriculum, which operates as an assault on the condition and concerns of working class women. Sexist jokes are common, women-hating thinly disguised as academic argument is rife, sexual harassment is usual. Men monopolise discussions, discuss and trivialise women's contributions, share jokes and allegiances with other men at women's expense and in just the same way as Spender[12] observed in schools, become troublesome and aggressive if they and their concerns are not treated as central in the educational exchange. In my own experience women staff frequently come in for the same kind of treatment both in private, in staff meetings and academic boards and in the classroom, women are taken much less seriously, challenged more aggressively and we are made to feel we should work a whole lot harder than our male counterparts to demonstrate our right to intrude upon the territory of men. Academic machismo at its worst is just a more rarified variety of the competitiveness, bravado and bullying which typifies men's behaviour generally. Directed at women it has the effect of keeping us out of the labour movement, out of the pubs and clubs and off the streets. In higher education it contributes a number of the messages which might also lead us to suppose that, here too, our presence is unwelcome.

Institutions of higher education make few concessions to mature students and even less to mothers. Creche and nursery provisions are limited and expensive and do nothing to solve the problem of school age children after school, children who are off school sick, or in half-terms and holidays. Lectures, tutorials and seminars are arranged to suit the logic of the timetable and the convenience of the institution, rather than the domestic responsibilities of the students. Women students, if they are married, need their husbands' signature (*in loco parentis!*) on grant application forms, whilst single parents can be asked to prove that their dependent children are legitimate before they can be counted for grant assessment. Women who go into higher education without formal qualifications are reliant upon discretionary grants. At least two students of ours have been refused grants for the first year of university degree courses – effectively preventing their participation – because they have already completed 13 weeks TOPS courses. One woman, who had to retake her final examinations, was threatened with court action if she didn't repay her final year's grant. She had spent three years supplementing its meagre provision by part-time factory work in the evenings – writing her essays in the early hours of the morning and often existing on only two or three hours of sleep at night. To avoid the retribution of the courts she was forced to put her child into care so that she could work full-time to pay off the debt to the local authority. Another woman, after two terms of continuing struggle with staff and fellow-students on a pre-degree course who made jokes about battered women and poverty and feminism, and in which the general logic of the curriculum seemed to require them to learn, among other things, the Russian language as well as 400 years of European history and the main principles of surveying, gave up, feeling that she was both the wrong sex and the wrong class and in the wrong place. Since her husband had to be threatened with divorce proceedings by a solicitor's letter if he didn't sign the grant form in the first place, he took great delight in refusing to pay it back when she too was threatened with legal action. She borrowed the money from her mother.

Of course institutions of higher education will claim that the vagaries of grant provision are nothing to do with them and that any deficiencies are the responsibility of the local authorities. Looked at from the standpoint of working class women, however, the discretionary and punitive way in which limited financial assistance is provided represents just another mechanism in the apparatus of control which makes their presence in the system feel precarious.

Recently a tutor on the social work course at Southampton University advised women on Second Chance not to bother applying to be social workers unless they could prove to him at the interview that they had enough money to pay for 24-hour child care and no domestic problems which were likely to interfere with their studies. He commented, somewhat flippantly, that a husband earning £35,000 a year would help enormously.

In almost every other respect women who embark on courses without men fare better than those who have to square what they're doing with husbands, partners or lovers. Men who re-enter education as mature students probably need to make some adjustments too, but it is unlikely that their initiative is seen as anything other than important by their wives and children. Working class women's return to education – if it is tolerated at all – is only usually condoned if nothing noticeable changes at home. Women still retain the major responsibility for child care and domestic work and often feel they have to 'do it even better' so that their absence at college doesn't become a major source of grievance. This means that academic work has to be fitted in after domestic responsibilities have been seen to be done – in practice late at night or in the early hours of the morning. However, grievances are common – mostly to do with men feeling threatened by the prospect of their wives outstripping them. One woman on our programme had to fix up an interview at the polytechnic to which she was applying for her husband to do a course too, so that he could be persuaded to agree to her application. The matter wasn't so easily resolved, however, since she was accepted and he wasn't. He then began a relentless campaign of obstruction and resistance until she was finally persuaded to give up. Another began an OU degree so that he could have the same letters after his name as his wife. Another started applying for jobs in other parts of the country as soon as she was accepted and he has now succeeded in removing her from the source of his anxiety. Another – unable to believe that his wife is doing something for herself, or being taken seriously as a student – is convinced that she is having an affair and has persisted in following her about and questioning her about her movements. And these are not the men who burn books and tear up essays and threaten physical violence – although there are plenty of examples of them too.

In my experience the extent of academic understanding about the struggles women have at home to even arrive in the classroom – or any recognition that most of them will have done a half day's work at least before they come in the morning – is about as informed as a night at the movies watching 'Educating Rita' might be expected to make clear. The personal tutor role, whilst being a responsibility which some take seriously, is far too often viewed as an apology for good tutor-student relationships and is not at all seen as a priority by most teaching staff. Mature women students very quickly learn that their personal problems are their own business and that they are irrelevant to the academic exchange. They should be endured or resolved elsewhere. It would be comforting to present a picture of working class women highly attuned to the gross insensitivity, ignorance and complacency about all of this, which is typical of higher education, and taking on the prejudices, campaigning for changes and battling their way through to some kind of political achievement. And of course some women do, on their own often, overcoming considerable obstacles and without a lot of support from their nearest and dearest. They register their objection to the attitudes and values which they encounter. They get punished for it too, by being publicly ridiculed often, or having their work dismissed as polemics. It's all part of the shaping up and dressing down that goes on in the process of incorporation.

You might want to believe that their experiences on courses like Second Chance prepare them spiritually and politically for the battle. Sometimes it helps in terms of validating their outrage and being there to pick up the pieces as they get systematically smashed into submission. But Second Chance itself – a thirty week course spread over a year – a mere 120 hours to change a lifetime – with resources for 60 women that are less than the cost of putting one public school boy through a year at Winchester College – and in a social and a political climate which is not conducive to women stepping out of line, has an enormous – some would say impossible – balance to redress. The fact that any women at all gain courage and strength and the will to make changes is remarkable – but they do. Victories for women are achieved despite the education system not because of it. For many others the confidence to attribute blame to the system rather than deficiency to themselves has been obliterated by a lifetime of learning to turn anger inwards and not to expect very much for themselves. The experience of learning together with other working class women on Second Chance, and in an atmosphere which is woman-centred and woman-positive, and in which shared experiences of oppression take on a political dimension, can produce a different kind of analysis and a different kind of response. But studying on your own, in the very midst of the patriarchy, with centuries of tradition and privilege and powers to lend authority – it is enormously difficult to feel anything other than overwhelmed. In these circumstances it is more common to attribute learning difficulties to personal inadequacies rather than bad teaching. It is easier to turn a blind eye to sexist innuendo than speak out against it. It is more comfortable to keep your head down than to deliver it on a silver platter to the enemy. The reward for good behaviour might be a degree – which might secure a job – which might bring economic independence – which might make a difference. It might then be possible to think of working for other women. More likely, the institution will have achieved its intention of incorporating a few more potential rebels and distracting them from their rebellious ideas as an example to the rest. Or even more likely, women will return to exactly the same kinds of low-paid, insecure jobs which they did before, feeling a failure because they have not achieved more, and dissatisfied because they have been led to expect it.

With the odds stacked against them from the start it takes considerably more than a degree in sociology or cultural studies for working class women to change their world – let alone anybody else's.

Notes and References

1. For a discussion of 'really useful knowledge' see Richard Johnson, 'Really Useful Knowledge: Radical Education and Working Class Culture' in Clarke, Critcher and Johnson (eds) *Working Class Culture*, (Hutchinson, 1979). And for an application of the argument to women's education, see Jane L. Thompson, *Learning Liberation: Women's Response to Men's Education*, (Croom Helm, 1983).
2. The other essays in this collection are a further illustration of this point.
3. See Dale Spender, *Invisible Women: the Schooling Scandal*, (Writers and Readers Publishing Co-operative, 1982) who uses the tcrm about schooling. It can usefully be applied to the education system generally.
4. See Spender ibid. and also Dale Spender (ed.) *Men's Studies Modified*, (Pergamon Press, 1981).
5. It is comforting and usual in everyday discussions to attach great hope to the process of education as a way of changing attitudes and outdated behaviour patterns. There is no evidence that the education system in itself can change society however.
6. See Eileen Byrne *Women and Education* (Tavistock, 1978).
7. See *Learning Liberation* op. cit.
8. See Geoff Brown, 'Independence and Incorporation: The Labour College Movement and the WEA Before the Second World War' in Jane L Thompson (*ed.*) *Adult Education for a Change*, (Hutchinson, 1980).
9. See *Learning Liberation* op. cit. Chap. 5.
10. Beatrix Campbell, *Wigan Pier Revisited*, (Virago, 1984).
11. See *Learning Liberation* op. cit. Chap. 10.
12. *Invisible Women* op. cit.

Adult education and the women's movement

(Originally published in *Radical Approaches to Adult Education: A Reader*, ed Tom Lovett, Routledge 1988)

This essay illustrates the connection which Thompson frequently chose to draw between the women's movement and adult education as a social movement. By the late eighties she concedes that adult education has been forced to pay attention to the demands of the women's movement – but mostly in ways which either reinforce notions of women as victims of their own inadequacies or as potential customers for more radical kinds of courses. She notes the incorporation of the 'acceptable face of liberal feminism' into the programmes of most providers to cater for 'the feminist market' – but with little further intention to change the curriculum or structure of what remains within more mainstream provision.

Politically the patriarchal and economic backlash against feminism in the eighties was enormous, at a time when the women's movement was trying to deal with issues of difference (class, 'race', sexuality, disability) within its own analysis of oppression and practice. As many of the gains made by feminism in the late sixties and seventies came under attack from the consequence of Thatcherism and the ideology of post-feminism, Thompson was at her most radical about the need for separate education within the direction and control of women themselves. This was always a minority view in adult education, in which women-only provision (when it had feminist – as distinct from domestic – intentions) was usually negotiated as a 'confidence building' and 'remedial' activity. But not so in the philosophy and practice of Thompson. She has always been clear that for women serious, woman-centred education represents the intellectual dimension of the struggle for women's liberation. Its purpose is to raise consciousness, develop theories, clarify understanding and inform women's action for social change.

Adult education and the women's movement

For women, the re-emergence of feminism in the late 1960s has been one of the most important political developments since the war. Some women would want to link this with the consolidation of black consciousness and with the reclassification of lesbianism as a political and sexual choice rather than a congenital affliction. Others would mention the Peace Movement and an opposition to imperialism as related issues. Even women, who for a whole variety of familiar reasons, do not call themselves feminists, know that whatever else women's liberation means, it represents a standpoint that begins with women and with the intention of reconstituting the world for women as a better place. In terms of the distribution of the world's resources we know that women – half of the world's population – share 1 per cent of them.[1] And whilst this massive imbalance has an enormous amount to do with international capitalism, imperialism, racism and militarism, it is also embedded in the historical development of patriarchy which precedes all other oppressions, post-dates fascist, socialist and communist revolutions, and seems to recognise no boundaries when it comes to cultural, regional and ethnic differences. It is not only that patriarchy is institutionalised in the major systems and apparatus of control in any given society, but it also structures the interpersonal relationships between men and women in their private and most intimate concerns.

The re-emergence of feminism in the 1960s is important for women because, whatever other political struggles we might be engaged in, our subordination to men individually and collectively is a condition we share with all women irrespective of class, 'race' and sexual preference.

In the 1960s feminism was a fairly middle class affair. Some would say it still is – except that in Britain, just as in the earlier suffrage, trade union and legal struggles around the turn of the century, working class women had been strongly involved in campaigns to do with working conditions and wages, male violence, racism, childcare, housing and community action. Although a rich resource for trivialisation by the media, the women's movement in the 1970s succeeded in making issues to do with women's rights visible in ways they had not been for over sixty years. The launching of the United Nations Decade for Women began in Britain with the passing of Equal Pay and Anti-Sex Discrimination legislation, and so long as women's demands were not seen as too extreme, and were easily satisfied by a few minor modifications in the administration of sexual injustice, then the liberal socialist establishment seemed happy to make the appropriate gestures.

The main concerns of the women's movement at that time – job opportunities, pay, childcare, education and reproductive rights – were familiar topics of discussion and there was a sense in which ideas and attitudes were settling and shifting into more enlightened grooves. But, of course, not all feminists were happy to settle for gestures or liberal attitudes without much serious commitment to social change. The New Left was in practice turning out to be almost as bad as the Old Left when it came to defining political priorities and treating women as the cheer-leaders, nurturers and sexual services brigade of the revolution. By which time the sexual revolution was also wearing a bit thin and became more to do with increasing women's availability to men than the sexual autonomy and control over our own bodies we had all been promised. And when the economy began to collapse and the political optimism of the 1960s and early 1970s began to tarnish, it was women who saw our jobs, our wages, our support services and our educational opportunities become the first and most serious casualties of the new depression.

Of course, no one else except feminists and women [who were] returned to the trenches and put under seige noticed what was happening. Returned to the invisibility of the home front, where we should have been all along, unaccounted for among the statistics of unemployment, stuck with the main responsibility for unpaid community care as the welfare state collapsed, women have seen the major characteristics of the depression of the 1980s depicted as male and youth unemployment, the destruction of men's jobs, small businessmen going bankrupt and resentment turning to violence on the streets. Women's response to poverty and unemployment remains an enigma, and whilst the inequality which leads to civil war between men on the streets is called a riot, the battles at home between unequals, in which the less powerful are also the losers, is dismissed as 'domestic violence'.

In these circumstances the voice of feminism has become more insistent and more angry on behalf of battered and abused women and against male violence in general. Increasingly patriarchy, racism and militarism have been named as the main enemies rather than the milder rebukes of the 1970s against red tape, prejudice and sexism.

And women have become more impatient with each other for allowing the divisions which men have created historically – class, racism and heterosexuality – to continue to divide us as women and from preventing us of finding ways of working politically that do not only liberate women but transform the systems of oppression themselves. Not surprisingly, the popular trivialisation of the women's movement in the 1960s and 1970s has now sharpened into a more concentrated and vicious backlash against feminism. The return of women to the homefront to live in varying degrees of poverty has been paralleled by an intensification of family-centred propaganda to remind us that women are the 'natural' homemakers, and that in difficult and unsettled times our prime responsibility is to make sure that our men and our children and our dependent relatives are properly cared for. Feminist ideas are presented as extreme, and women who hold them are described variously as unfeminine, man-hating, aggressive, ugly and perverted. In circumstances in which women's primary commitment to men can no longer be guaranteed, the attack on 'extremists', and especially lesbians, within the women's movement has increased. It is part of an attempt to deter potential recruits and to distract us from concluding that it is men who are the cause of women's oppression, not anyone else.[2] On top of all of this I now read in my newspaper that we are living in 'the post-feminist era' which I take to mean either that the battle is won – a view based on the same kind of stupidity which once encouraged Macmillan to proclaim 'we're all middle class now' – or that feminism is a spent force and has slipped back into obscurity for another sixty years of oblivion. Either way the notion is both ill-informed and ridiculous, and demonstrates the dangers of paying too much attention to newspapers like *The Guardian*.

So far as adult education is concerned, it would seem reasonable to expect some significant response to the women's movement, given the close association between adult education and popular political movements in the formative years, and also because women constitute the majority of students in current adult education provision. In practice, of course, this hasn't been the case, largely because the controlling influence in adult education historically, and those who monopolise the current debate and the definitions of issues in adult education, are mostly men. This is not the place to elaborate upon why the educational system we have inherited can be described as men's education or why, even in areas like adult and community education in which women outnumber men as students, and are employed in considerable numbers as part-time tutors and volunteers, the structures in which we operate are still so effectively grounded in male power and male values as to appear inevitable.[3] Except to say that women's entry into education generally was conceded reluctantly and belatedly a hundred or so years ago, long after the rules had been established and the parameters had been set. Our subsequent participation has been conditional upon our acceptance of the inevitable – a curriculum constructed historically as a reflection of men's ideas, assumptions and priorities, presented as objective truth: and a view of women informed by a range of ideologies collectively based upon notions of male supremacy. For women, education in the men's system has meant learning a lot about men in male ways and a lot about learning to be the women men have determined we should be.

In adult education, more than in schooling, and more than in higher education, the possibilities for resisting the inevitable are greater, because the learning relationship is not based on compulsion in quite the same way, and because there is less male power invested in it. And yet the evidence of radical initiatives on behalf of women, which seriously challenge patriarchal knowledge and control, actually being seen to flourish and transform oppressive structures, are extremely rare. Most of what passes for women's education, and which is considered different in kind and emphasis from that which is usually provided in mainstream education for women, is, in my view, a transparent variation on a familiar theme. In circumstances in which the opinion leaders and policy-makers in adult education have responded to the women's movement at all, it has been to co-opt feminism into their platitudes, whilst at the same time seeking to deflect and defeat the radical intention of women's liberation as it might be applied in adult education and society generally.

If we examine the record of adult education in relation to the women's movement there seem to me to be four kinds of responses. The most familiar is that of total ignorance, in the sense of making no response at all, and which could also be said to be based on total ignorance.

The second is based on a latter day philanthropy, which like its nineteenth-century antecedent, muffles the iron fist of control in the velvet glove of sentiment. This kind of response is based on the view that women are one of those 'minorities' (sic) who are disadvantaged and for whom the mission of adult education is to provide the wherewithal to cope with their misfortunes.

The third response is more enlightened and less grounded in the liberal fixation with genetic and pathological explanations of deficiency when it comes to deprivation. But it still retains the liberal tradition of 'rescue' in its definition of responsibility. This response has incorporated the respectable face of feminism, concerned with 'equal rights', into its understanding and provision, with a range of initiatives intended to acknowledge the justice of equal opportunities. It is favoured by all those who believe that institutional practices can be changed by persistence and goodwill, and by those who understand that the best way to defeat feminism is to co-opt its radical and rebellious potential.

The fourth response is more to do with the response of the women's movement to adult education than the other way round, and about welcoming adult education as just one more arena in the battle for women's liberation. It is based on the conviction that women's liberation is principally about personal and social change, but that the opportunity for consciousness raising and intellectual clarification of ideas and strategies, together with the consolidation that can come from collective support and struggle, constitutes 'really useful knowledge' in the old radical sense of the term.[4] But it is not simply the nature of knowledge that matters in this view of women's education; it is control over the learning process. Radical feminists want freedom from male control. It is this version of the relationship between adult education and the women's movement which is at the same time the most challenging and the most precarious.

Total ignorance

It has taken a long time for those engaged in mainstream adult education to attribute any significance to the Women's Movement whatsoever. A few years ago, in the brief period of enthusiasm and expansion after Russell, those responsible for writing reports, conducting research and making recommendations, did so in the fairly jovial, cavalier fashion that could be said to characterise the type of men who operated their way to the top in adult education. If the old guard could be depicted as slightly fusty quasi-academics, the 'new boys', who became the opinion leaders in the 1970s, with their retinue of henchmen and clones at local level, were more populist in their manner and opportunist in their principles. The inheritors of the liberal tradition, they reconstituted its principles and practice to legitimise their entrepreneurial concern to extend the influence of adult education, to manage and professionalise the service, and to advance their own importance. All of this with no reference made to one of the most significant, popular, grassroots political movements of the time – feminism.[5]

Despite the fact that the majority of students in adult education are women, the majority of volunteers, part-time workers, detached workers, and assistant workers in adult education are women, those with key jobs in the career structure – mostly men – made no recognition of this fact, except in so far as it influenced their assumptions about 'relevant' curricula and enabled them to plan programmes which depended upon an enormous amount of female exploitation. In terms of their publications, their journal contributions, their conference papers, their committees and planning groups, women's existence and participation were both invisible and tokenistic. Just as it was extremely difficult to get the liberal establishment to take on board issues to do with social class in the 1970s[6] so too was it rare to hear feminism and the politics of gender discussed with any degree of seriousness or attention at any of their gatherings.

Today, the response based on total ignorance is still alive and well in circumstances in which even the limited attention given to gender discrimination in schools far exceeds its identification as an issue in the provision of educational opportunities for adult women. Most LEA programmes and the mainstay of WEA and extra-mural provision remains locked into the restricted notion of women as homemakers, or as consumers of male culture and ideas. As ever vigilant assessors of needs, and assiduous entrepreneurs in the pursuit of punters, the rhetoric in practice turns out to be predictably familiar across regional and social settings. It is not unusual, for example, to find adult education centres in the middle of inner cities, where the inhabitants are generally poor and from a variety of ethnic backgrounds, providing the kind of curriculum which remains a testimony to white, petit-bourgeois aspirations and hobbies, peopled by students who travel into classes by car, from outside the immediate neighbourhood. Those who operate according to total ignorance about the women's movement also pay scant attention to social class and 'race' as critical concerns in the content and teaching and provision of what passes as adult education.

Under pressure from government economic policies and spending cuts, the predisposition to rethink conventional provision is slight, except in so far as as competition for student numbers, effective teaching hours and fee-income intensifies the concentration on popular recreational and leisure pursuits, rather than innovative and developmental work in areas which cannot be relied upon to be lucrative.

The picture in extra-mural departments and the WEA is much the same, as the liberal tradition fights a rearguard collapse in the name of 'education for its own sake' in the face of enormous government and institutional pressure to become cost-effective. In these circumstances there is little visible money to be made out of feminism as such, although there are specific financial benefits to be gained by institutions from the identification of women as a deprived minority.

Latter day philanthropy

One of the achievements of the British ruling class historically has been its capacity to deflect opposition and resistance by calculated philanthropy and by the concentration on individualism as an explanation of success and failure. It is less important that people gain sustenance from philanthropic benevolence than that gestures are seen to be made. It matters little whether there is much evidence of individualism creating success or failure so long as it is believed that it does. It is important, if the interests and privileges of the ruling class are to be preserved, that not too many people develop a sense of grievance, outrage or anger about the inequalities and oppressions which they experience. It is also important that agencies like education, the media, government and the legal system assist the ruling class in preserving those interests. Great care has been taken in the current depression, for example, to construct the image of scrounging, fiddling, laziness and greed as characteristic of the unemployed who 'could find work if they really wanted to' or whose misfortune can be explained by 'the irresponsible pay demands and restrictive practices' of those still in work. The nineteenth-century notion of the undeserving poor and the deserving poor has been reconstituted – the former are effectively stigmatised, the latter become the focus of qualified liberal sentiment – the target group for crumbs of philanthropic consideration. Benevolence becomes the bridge between oppression and control.

The proliferation of these views in adult education is based not on a class or 'race' or gender analysis of inequality but on notions of feckless, unconfident, incompetent individuals who, because of 'learning difficulties' or lack of 'social and life skills', are inadequate in their day-to-day lives. They are seen not as the victims of social problems but as those who contribute to their own victimisation by their irresolution or fatalism or apathy. In the 'post-feminist era', equal opportunities are available to those women who 'get off their hands and knees and work for them'. Those who don't 'have only themselves to blame'. In the 1970s such individuals were called 'educationally' and 'emotionally deprived' or 'culturally disadvantaged', and a whole quasi-medical terminology of concern and cure became part of the intervention procedure of community workers, social workers and educationalists.[7] Today, the same individuals have become labelled as minority groups – ethnic, unemployed and women whose 'special needs' are the focus of limited intervention by the 'caring professions' including adult education.

Women who are identified as a problem are those whose isolation and poverty and poor housing affects their competence in childcare, domestic skills and coping with unsatisfactory circumstances. The cure? More domestication. Adult education's concern for them is mediated through community education outreach schemes based in neighbourhoods, community centres, clinics and mother and toddler groups. The emphasis is on contact and a chance to talk, on non-formal activities centring on children, domestic skills and basic literacy. The philosophy underpinning such schemes is simplistic and patronising, concentrating on women's deficiencies rather than their strengths, their inadequacies rather than their capacities, their limitations rather than their possibilities. Education is rarely named by providers for fear of alienation and women are talked about in ways which make the hairs on the back of your neck stand on end. The role of the teacher/outreach worker is to guide, facilitate, contain, but not to engage in critical social analysis or action. Although frequently the recipients of special grants, such schemes are understaffed and poorly funded, given the enormity of the resources which would be needed if women in such groups were to be genuinely compensated for their massive economic disadvantage and their political powerlessness. The schemes are also usually only short-term – six months, a year, two years at the most. But then, the intention is not to solve social problems so easily, only to acknowledge them. The recent history of the liberal response to urban deprivation as it affects groups like women is littered with the unmet commitments and unfulfilled promises of such initiatives: each highly circumscribed; each mediated through the transitory commitment of part-time interlopers in communities in which they do not live, among women whose lives they do not share; and all controlled elsewhere. The best thing that can be said of them is that their contact with women is slight, the numbers who participate regularly are few, and whilst this reinforces the commonsense definition of poverty as being a result of apathy, it protects those who escape from the prescriptions of unperceptive need-meeters and from yet more management by misguided missionaries.

Equally, fashions in philanthropy change. The social isolation of women is not nearly as popular a cause for concern as it was in the 1970s. More recently, unemployment or what now gets euphemistically referred to as 'education for leisure' has become the flavour of the month. In practice this means men.

The respectable face of feminism
Of course, many workers in adult education are also feminists – they may be the anti-sexist male variety – but on the whole they are women who want adult education to respond to the concerns of the women's movement. (Whatever happened to liberation?) Adult education, unencumbered by the constraints of certification and examination, has been a popular breeding-ground for courses which focus on women's cultural and political ideas and activities. Workshops, day schools, short and more intensive courses about women's literature and history and psychology and health, for example, have become a feature of every self-respecting liberal studies programme; whilst courses in self-defence, assertiveness training, women's sexuality, welfare rights, peace studies and feminist politics have helped to reconstitute what is usually defined as a relevant curriculum for women. In the LEA sector women have been able to learn non-traditional skills like building, carpentry, motor mechanics and electrics. Some courses, especially those sponsored by the Manpower Services Commission (MSC) like Wider Opportunities for Women, have been concerned with women re-entering the labour market. Others, like New Opportunities for Women, have provided the re-entry points into higher and continuing education for women whose choices have been restricted by marriage and childcare and lack of opportunity. The growth and development of new technologies and scientific knowledge have inspired programmes providing positive discrimination for women in areas concerned with science and computing. Some, encouraged by the Equal Opportunities Commission (EOC) have offered Women into Accounting, Women into Management and Women into Public Life courses, aimed at women trying to break into areas of employment and influence usually

monopolised by men. The variety is enormous as is the nature of the response to feminism which they reflect.

The characteristic that courses for career women, courses reclaiming the curriculum on behalf of women's history and culture, and courses providing useful knowledge and skills for women reconstituting their traditional roles have in common is the recognition that some women at least have expectations, aspirations and preoccupations which are not well catered for in the mainstream provision of adult education. The assumption remains that most women will continue to be satisfied with conventional provision and that the others, the 'more liberated' perhaps, can choose women's studies options which now exist amidst the many other courses that go to make up a centre programme. The attraction of this approach is that most up-to-date and enlightened LEA centres, WEA branches and extra-mural departments can be relied upon to include some kind of women's studies in their provision which is different in kind from domestic education and men's education.

The problem with this approach, however, is that it is so often based on opportunism rather than commitment. So long as women's studies options exist, the rest of the curriculum which is not women's studies, and the structures in which knowledge is constructed, managed and transmitted, can remain unchanged. Issues about who comes to adult education, what knowledge gets transmitted, how the teaching-learning relationship is negotiated, who is in control, are all just as important questions for feminist education as the introduction of feminist content and analysis into the curriculum of some courses. And yet these are issues which the token recognition paid to the women's movement in adult education does not even begin to consider. The contradiction remains that in a liberal framework, feminism can be tolerated in a piecemeal way, and be claimed as evidence of enlightenment and progress, so long as nothing else – the rest – has to change.

Another problem with this view of reality is that it is more likely to respond to the respectable face of feminism than to women's liberation. So far as I am concerned, the conviction that women's studies is about management training and courses to help women to be more assertive and successful in public life (like Margaret Thatcher?), doesn't have very much to say about how the majority of women live our lives. Courses which substitute female content for male content in the curriculum, but which continue to fragment subjects, which reflect the same criteria about what counts as excellence, and which construct language and theories which are obscure and elitist, all echo patriarchal ways of learning.

Just because courses are attended by women, taught by women and are about women, does not in itself make them feminist. With an educational heritage created and sustained by men, and in a context in which men control the employment of teachers and the allocation of resources, the constraints are enormous. In these circumstances the politics of penetration becomes the art of the possible. Women modify their demands and their language and explain their intentions in terms which will seem reasonable. Obvious flashpoints like 'women-only classes' and 'separatist politics' are avoided and terminology likely to be alarming like 'lesbianism', 'patriarchy', 'woman hating' and 'liberation', is diluted into 'sexuality', 'inequality of opportunity', 'sexism' and 'equal rights'. The price of a foothold in the system is compromise. The struggle, once a tiny space has been achieved, is to stay put. This can mean more compromise. The danger of compromise of course is that you forget what's been relinquished in the pursuit of what's been achieved. The vision is translated into consequences which seem possible. The possible is dictated by the limits of men's tolerance. Men's intolerance is fortified by their power.

Some of the compromise has to do with money. Defined as a 'minority group' with 'special needs', women's courses can attract – in adult education terms – quite large grants of money and special funding, principally from the European Social Fund (ESF) and MSC. European funding can be lavish but it is tied to cooperation with public bodies. Grants are not given into the control of women participating in the projects being funded. A more common relationship is that between adult education and MSC whose declared commitment to training of various kinds and social education in preparation for responsible citizenship is well known. The philosophy underlying the operation of MSC is also well known. It is rooted in conservative values of limited self-help, virtuous thrift and individualism. Courses can be instrumental or diversionary but not contentious. Students, tutors and the curriculum are supervised by representatives of MSC and unnecessary luxuries like creches attached to women's courses are conspicuous by their absence 'in case women become dependent upon support services that will not be provided in the wider society'. MSC are opposed to schemes which can be defined by them as political or critical of prevailing government policy – in practice, this leaves courses for women which concentrate on traditional job skills and traditional job expectations – even though those skills are not valued in the present economic climate and the new opportunities for women in the labour market are negligible.

Dependency on short-term grants and external funding is an excellent way of keeping women – as well as other disadvantaged groups – in competition with each other for scarce resources. So long as the energies of project workers and project participants can be distracted by the relentless search for short-term funding, the chances of any significant changes being achieved are minimal. Also, this form of poverty control and management is most susceptible to applications intended to pacify potentially disorderly groups. Projects directed at cooling the anger of the male unemployed or blacks in inner city areas are likely to be more successful than schemes seeking to increase women's access to employment or educational opportunities.

The picture so far presented, of feminism being restrained by this form of response to the women's movement, is not completely accurate, however. There are women holding positions of influence in adult education who have used their power to secure space and resources for women which would not otherwise exist. The consolidation of women's visibility and conspicuous presence in adult education means that the men with power must take us into account in ways which otherwise would not happen. In organisations like the WEA particularly, because of its grass roots and more democratic base, women have been able to take more control of their own learning and become their own teachers and organise themselves in ways which are less controlled by patriarchal infiltration. Although, as money runs out, the cost-effectiveness of non-traditional classes comes under greater scrutiny. For feminists who believe in coalition with other progressive groups, and in the power of eloquence to change men's attitudes, then educational systems, like other institutions, can become the site of struggle in which concerted action might bring about changes in personnel and policies. It may be in these circumstances that moderation rather than liberation is more likely to achieve results, but it is a matter of interpretation whether the results achieved by good behaviour are worth the energy required. When feminism becomes respectable – and if the world hasn't been turned upside down as a consequence – the significance of our achievements needs to be examined carefully.

Freedom from men's control

There isn't a great deal of historical precedent to support the view that patriarchy can be transformed by sweet reason and persuasion. It is more likely that the incorporation of radical ideas will contribute to their dilution and distraction. The definitions attached to strategies for change in educational institutions, as in other institutions, to do with becoming effective lobbyists, operators and competitors, are based on assumptions constructed over time about politics and power. Men have practised and perfected these strategies for centuries in different contexts. They may disagree with each other profoundly, and compete to outdo each other relentlessly, but they share the same notion of the contest and adhere, more or less, to the same rules. A change of emphasis merely replaces one group of men by another, as does revolution. The method is as much a creation of their history and culture as is the priority given to the issues they compete about. Women wedded to men's systems, arguing for resources and significance, have little alternative but to accept the context as given and learn as effectively as possible, to pitch in with the rest. The problem with this, of course, is that, as in most sports, some competitors are nobbled from the start. They can never win, and when it looks like they might, someone moves the goal post. The odds against women beating men at their own game, without becoming amateur men in the process, are enormous. Access to men's institutions, without the transformation of the ways in which they operate, will not in itself assist women's struggle for independence. Given the resources available to men (99 percent of the world's resources) and the few available to women, and given the institution of male power in every dimension of the education system – grounded deep in the structures, the language and the social context of every exchange – it is unrealistic to imagine that individual women, men of good will, or students, however energetic, resourceful and determined, can change things single-handed. If it were merely a matter of eloquence, or energy or conviction, the education system, like other male institutions, would have been transformed by women already. It's like expecting the class system to change once the workers have explained to the ruling class why they don't like poverty; or racism to go away once blacks have made clear why they find it oppressive.

Much better as women to put our energies elsewhere and to think in terms of guerilla action – to redistribute resources to women wherever possible; to asset-strip men's buildings of their space and facilities and resources on behalf of women; to expose male hypocrisy, corruption and oppression wherever it appears; to reserve loyalty for principles and for women not for institutions; and to concentrate on the subversion of men's ideas about themselves and about women by behaving badly and with irreverence to their rules. Adrienne Rich puts it precisely:

> *The question facing women's studies today is the extent to which she has, in the last decade, matured into the dutiful daughter of the white patriarchal university – a daughter who threw tantrums and played the tomboy when she was younger, but who has now learned to wear a dress and speak and act almost as nicely as Daddy wants her to. And the extent to which women's studies can remember that her mother was not Athena, but the Women's Liberation Movement, a grass roots political movement with roots in the civil rights movement of the 1960s; a movement blazing with lesbian energy whose earliest journals had names like, **It Ain't Me Babe, No More Fun and Games, Off Our Backs, Up From Under** and **The Furies**. In other words, how disobedient will women's studies be in the 1980s? And how will she address the racism, misogyny, homophobia of the university and of the corporate society in which it is embedded? And how will feminist teachers and scholars choose to practise their disobedience to white patriarchy?*[8]

An education which does justice to feminist priorities is not merely a matter of curriculum innovation and change although when women begin to rewrite the history and culture of societies in ways which include the diversity of women's experiences, and when women generate their own knowledge and become their own teachers – the consequences can be challenging to men's view of the world and their view of women. It is common to dismiss women's analysis and writing as tendentious, irrational, subjective, misguided, or more simply wrong. What it means, of course, is that very often we have different definitions of experience and reality from men, and that much of what we say is critical of men and about what they have done to women. Because of this, the Second Chance for Women courses[9] in Southampton have been continually investigated by local politicians, LEA advisers, university professors and HMIs for signs of bias, indoctrination and extremism in ways which other courses sponsored by the university department have never been. And despite the lip-service paid to 'experimental learning' and 'Freirian praxis' in the rhetoric of some opinion leaders, this frequently omits any concerted effort to make space for feminist ideas in adult education. Increasingly, it has been necessary in Southampton to think in terms of creating our own learning environment in a separate Women's Education Centre in which men as students, teachers or visiting authorities are unwelcome and in which women act independently for themselves. The rationale for women-only classes in adult education is often explained as a remedial exercise, in terms of women's lack of confidence and men's tendency to dominate and monopolise the educational exchange. Whilst this is undoubtably true – men, even when they're in the minority, take up proportionally more space and time and attention[10] than in equity they are entitled to – but it is not the reason why radical feminists argue for their exclusion. The most effective way in which any group, conscious of its oppression and concerned to change the relationships of oppression,

can organise, is without the participation of the oppressors in the process of resistance. It is also empowering for groups who have long been powerless, downgraded,
humiliated, patronised, deskilled and diminished to discover the strength of concerted
action for themselves and on their own behalf. The same can be said for working-
class, black and other oppressed groups. It is as true in political campaigns like
Greenham and against male violence as it is in the reconstruction of an education
which serves the concerns, reflects the values, and enhances the priorities of women.
It means also the creation of a different kind of education in which the organisation
and control is with women and in which the usual demarcation between teachers
and learners, thought and action, fact and feelings, personal and public, becomes
removed. It is not, on the whole, the kind of shift which men in education take
kindly to. It challenges their authority and specialisms and notions of objectivity. It
also raises critical questions about purpose: for example, is the purpose of education
to consolidate the logic of the present system or is it to challenge and transform it?

The other reason why women should organise and educate separately is because
we have more important work to do than to have our attention and energy continually claimed by men. Merely surviving in male systems, let alone trying to challenge
them, is exhausting and frustrating in ways which drain energy away from more
important issues. The re-emergence of feminism, which began as a flash of vision,
and continued with an examination of the evils and gross distortions of patriarchy,
and led to a whole variety of campaigns on behalf of women, now needs to concentrate
on the differences between us as women which have divided us under patriarchy and
which cannot be allowed to divide us as feminists.

Contemporary divisions are based mainly on class, 'race', age, politics, disability and sexual identity; and of these class, 'race', and sexual identity are possibly
the most urgent in our immediate struggle.[11] Feminists who are also black, working-
class or lesbian (or all three) have been as concerned as any other group to establish
their own identity and to reclaim their own realities as women. But the women's
movement, especially as it is represented in western-style education, is dominated by
white, middle class, heterosexual women. It has not been sufficiently sensitive to the
issues which divide and potentially destroy us, or to the need to renounce the legacy
of patriarchal relations in our own behaviour. Statistics aren't necessary to document
what is painfully obvious. Working class women live in increasing poverty and are
more vulnerable than middle class women to state interference and control.[12] Black
women live and work in the poorest of circumstances and confront the penalties of
white racism as a matter of course in every aspect of their lives.[13] Lesbian women can
expect to lose their jobs, their children and their community support because they
choose to love women in preference to men.[14] Written in the kind of prose that in
itself contains the capacity to change women's lives, Audre Lorde reminds us of our
differences, and of the reasons why we need to overcome them:

> We are not as women living in a political and social vacuum. We operate in
> the teeth of a system for whom racism and sexism are primary, established,
> necessary props of profit . . . I am a lesbian woman of colour whose children
> eat regularly because I work in a university. If their full bellies make me fail

*to recognise my communality with a woman of colour whose children who do
not eat, because she can't find work; or a woman who has no children
because her insides are rotten from home abortions and sterilisation; or if I
fail to recognise the lesbian who chooses not to have children, or the woman
who remains closeted because her homophobic community is her only life
support; the woman who chooses silence instead of another death; the
woman who is terrified lest any anger triggers the explosion of hers; if I fail to
recognise these women as other faces of myself, then I am contributing to
each of their oppressions, but also to my own. I am not free while any
woman is unfree, even when her shackles are very different from my own.
Nor are you.*[15]

For the women's movement now this is one of the most important issues we have to
deal with – the solidarity of our relationships with each other and the eradication of
all the oppressions we have inherited from capitalist patriarchy. The other major
concern for women is about finding ways of living which give us more independence,
more control over our own lives, and more self worth than is frequently the experience of women in subordination to men.

Men's opposition to women-only education, as with other women-only activities, is the fear of separatism and of men's exclusion from influence and control in
our lives. This opposition, expressed in terms of adult education, seems out of all
proportion, given that most women can expect to spend at most three or four hours a
week in women-only classes as against a lifetime in the world of men. And yet men
do have reason to be concerned if, on these occasions, women find their lonely anger
or isolated oppression is understood and shared by other women, so that personal
struggles take on political dimensions. And if, in a woman-centred, woman-positive,
pro-woman environment, women discover their affiliation and affection for other
women, which raises critical questions about friendship and solidarity and love, and
why we spend so much time and emotional energy on relationships with men which
cause us so much pain.

Living and working separately from men, on our own, or with other women
and children, as a conscious political choice and labelled separatism is not something
the vast majority of women would identify as a possibility. It seems extreme and
many women, for reasons of poverty, children and physical fear remain in unsatisfactory relationships without hope of change. But yet, the steady increase in the divorce
rate over the last fifteen years or so is not the simple consequence of attending
women's studies classes. The fact that women remarry is not surprising. What is more
surprising, given the amount of pressure that goes into promoting compulsory
heterosexuality and married bliss, and given the economic and social penalties
imposed on single parenthood by the state, is that, increasingly, women are choosing
to bring up children on their own without close relationships with men. Many women
in this position today, sharing childcare and social support with other women, meeting in mother and toddler groups, in each other's houses, at the school gates, at the
shops, are engaged in a kind of separatism. They are experiencing what women have
always known – that the life-sustaining relationships that enable us to grit our teeth

and pick our way through the mess made by men, to endure and to survive, are those we share with other women: our mothers, our sisters, our neighbours and friends. I have yet to see much validation of this support women give each other, especially in working class communities, which recognise it as a political affiliation, a movement. It is more common to associate what counts as politics in such communities with the labour movement – a movement which men have created and in which men meet to decide priorities and strategies. It is however an important part of the women's movement, which might lack the explicit analysis of male oppression and resistance, but is none the less an affirmation of women's allegiance to each other. The problem is, that because of the power of male definitions of reality in our culture, and because women are taught to accept these definitions too, the friendship and support which countless women give to each other can remain unacknowledged and invisible. The structural organisation of women's isolation in the home compounded by women's poverty doesn't help. And yet once these connections are made visible and acknowledged often, in my experience, in the context of feminist education groups and meetings – the sense of men's significance evaporates. It becomes possible to imagine other ways of living. It becomes possible, if we remain committed to living and working with men, to identify the terms on which we shall agree to participate and what re-negotiation needs to go on if these relationships are to be transformed.

The argument for feminist education, free from male control, is not as a remedial excercise, it is because we have important work to do together, from which we cannot afford to be distracted by the interference and destruction we know happens when men remain in control.

True and false rebellion

The problem we face as feminists is to understand the difference between true and false rebellion. White capitalist patriarchy will allow a certain amount of argument and independent thought. 'Women's Lib' has matured and has become incorporated into the language and into the superficial behaviour of most self-respecting liberal socialists. A good many educated women have used the ideology of economic independence, job sharing and role swapping to establish careers which bring satisfaction and economic rewards. Many have become lifestyle feminists with husbands, partners and boyfriends who have cultivated the good humoured acceptance of feminist ideas and who behave as non-oppressive, anti-sexist men, cooking the ratatouille, organising creches at women's conferences, and turning a blind eye to untidy houses and piles of dirty washing. But this is not the experience of most black and working class women.

In the academy, where a semblance of pluralism persists, it is perfectly acceptable to introduce elements of Women's Studies material into the curriculum which, during the last fifteen years or so, has also made space for Black Studies, the teaching of 'race' relations and working class history. None of these has posed any particular threat to the hagemony of traditional discipline and patterns of academic thought and women can be incorporated as easily as the rest.

In all of these circumstances women can wear their feminist hearts on their sleeves and the world will continue much the same. It's only when women refuse to toe the line, when we renounce the rewards of good behaviour and resist all attempts to be incorporated, that true rebellion comes into its own. It is only when women cross the line drawn by patriarchy and choose to do things on our own and when our collusion with racism, homophobia and class oppression can no longer be guaranteed, that real resistance and real possibilities begin to emerge.

Notes and References

1. United Nations statistics. Women are one-half of the world's population, do two-thirds of the world's work, earn one-tenth of the world's wages and own one-hundredth of the world's wealth.

2. Although official figures consistently underestimate the true extent of male crimes of violence against women, it is well known that women and children are in more danger of domestic violence, rape and sexual abuse from male members of their own family than from strangers. The fears expressed by the general public about mugging, rape and child abuse are almost without exception a fear of men.

3. See Jane Thompson, *Learning Liberation: Women's Response to Men's Education* (Croom Helm, 1983).

4. Richard Johnson, "Really Useful Knowledge": Radical Education and Working-Class Culture, in Clarke Critcher and Johnson (eds), *Working Class Culture* (Hutchinson, 1979).

5. Thompson, op cit

6. The ideas of the 1970s opinion leaders are criticised in Jane Thompson (ed.), *Adult Education for a Change* (Hutchinson, 1980).

7. Ibid., Chapter 4.

8. Adrienne Rich, address to the National Women's Studies of America Annual Conference in June 1981.

9. Thompson, *Learning Liberation*, Chapter 10.

10. Dale Spender, *Man Made Language* (Routledge and Kegan Paul, 1980).

11. Thompson, *Learning Liberation*.

12. Beatrix Campbell, *Wigan Pier Revisited* (Virago, 1984).

13. Beverly Bryan, Stella Dadzie and Suzanne Scuse, *The Heart of the Race* (Virago, 1985).

14. *Lesbian Mothers on Trial* (Rights of Women, 1984)

15. Audre Lorde, address to the National Women's Studies of America Conference, June 1981.

Doing it for ourselves

(Originally published in *Learning the Hard Way:
Women's Oppression in Men's Education*,
with The Taking Liberties Collective, Macmillan 1989)

*'Doing It For Ourselves' was written by Thompson with the Taking Liberties
Collective as part of a joint writing project at the Women's Education Centre in
1988. It was published in the Macmillan Women in Society series in 1989. The
book draws on the writing of around fifty, mostly working class, women who were or
had been members of the Centre. As such it is a remarkable testimony in the
literature of adult education and women's studies – including poems, personal writing
and fragments of autobiography – to produce a well sustained argument, written by
those whose lives were touched and changed by their experience of women's education. Although not conventionally academic, the writing is powerful and moving, and
when used with students whose lives are connected through similar material and
political conditions, it continues to be a wonderful resource for hope and inspiration.
The book anticipates many of the arguments which educationalists and academics
were subsequently to make about the damage done by New Right policies to the lives
of poor people including women and about the challenges facing Women's Education
from liberal-therapeutic tendencies (associated with the WEA in the late eighties) and
from mainstreaming (associated with the access industry) as a strategy for entry into
higher education. In this passage the Collective describes the simple philosophy which
underpinned the organisation and practice of the Women's Education Centre
throughout the eighties.*

Doing it for ourselves

*A 'friend' told me the other day that I should have been born a man. She
was wrong of course. I don't want to be a man. I just want to be a plumber!*

In comparison to what we learned at school, and what some of us have learned from
traditional adult education or from entering higher education as 'mature students',
our experiences of women's education are altogether something else. Coming, for the
most part, from white, working-class backgrounds, it is unusual to find 'education' a
relevant or empowering experience. We know from the words of black women
included here, and from lengthy discussions with black sisters, that the chances of
black, working class women receiving anything of value from white, middle class
men's education are even more remote. With the education system so obviously geared
to the self interest and concerns of white, middle class men we have found no better
alternative than to take matters into our own hands and 'do it ourselves'.

Learning with other women with feminist intent implies a number of important
principles. They may seem obvious to those of you reading this book, but they are by
no means the common experience of most women returning to education. Together
they form the basis on which women's education concerned with women's liberation
should be based. Principles like women-only classes; a curriculum which is based on
women-centred knowledge; teaching-learning approaches which break down
hierarchies between 'experts' and 'others'; an atmosphere which discourages the
divisiveness of class privilege, racism and anti lesbianism; the validation of personal
experience; knowledge which is politically useful in the battle against patriarchy;
good childcare; flexible timing; minimal fees and freedom from male interference and
control.

Our starting point is obvious. Courses need to be arranged at times that fit in
with our domestic commitments.

*What is great about this course is that it is geared to the needs of women.
The hours are perfect for us with children at school – you've got enough time
to take them to school in the morning, and pick them up again in the
afternoon. And you don't have to worry about half-terms and holidays and
who you can get to look after them – we're off at the same time as the
schools.*

As we've seen, such considerations are the exception rather than the rule in most adult, further and higher education. It's also important that good creches are provided for women with pre-school age children. Not a box of broken toys and three schoolgirl volunteers in a makeshift space, but a well-run creche, with experienced workers who also have a political understanding of their educational responsibilities.

> *At the moment I am working in the Centre creche. We ensure that women with small children can enjoy courses knowing that their children are safe and having a good time. The creche exists not just as a place to leave the kids, but as a very important part of the Centre and its commitment to working in anti-sexist, anti-racist and anti-classist ways. Children are encouraged to explore and learn new tasks and experiences, and learn to play together in a sharing and co-operative way.*

At the Women's Education Centre (WEC) we have always placed a lot of emphasis on good creche provision and tried to make sure that workers are well paid and properly recognised for the important work they do.

> *The WEC is rightly proud of its creche. Few other educational institutions can provide one of such a high standard or so regularly. This is due to the efforts of women at the Centre who have given time and energy to its creation and operation – and still do so. Society deems creches to be an unnecessary luxury; not surprising since it values women only insofar as they reduce society's costs. But our creche is no luxury. It is a vital necessity for women to begin learning in a small space of their own, often preparing for a working life as a single parent in the future. Absence of a creche effectively relegates low-income mothers to the breadline for the future.*

It is also important in women's education that any fees charged for courses are kept to a minimum and easily waived. We know from our own experience that the majority of us could not have joined courses like Second Chance if we'd had to pay high fees.

> *I was only able to attend Second Chance because my fees were waived. Supplementary Benefit (now Income Support) does not recognise the 'luxury' of education for women. Education, however, should never be a luxury or a privilege, dependant on financial status. It must be a right. Any insistence that fees must be paid by women such as myself means that right is then withdrawn. The course helped me more than I can say, and it must remain open to all women regardless of their financial status. I am now doing a degree course. I owe that to some remarkable women who believed in me and not my cheque book.*

More often than not we are prevented from doing courses because we can't afford the fees.

> *We have always lived on a low income, so I could not afford the daytime courses offered in adult education and certainly could not find money for nurseries or childminders as well. I have never been able to get to evening*

classes because of the unsocial hours my husband works. I thoroughly resent
the fact that working class women like myself have such a hard time taking
advantage of the further education we are supposedly entitled to – those who
are able to obviously already have several advantages over me! I applaud
moves to run free courses for unemployed men, but I cannot understand why
the same principle should not be applied to women who are single parents, or
unwaged mothers or who are living on a low income.

For women with little money to call our own, arbitrary demands for cash as evidence
of our commitment to learning is grossly insulting.

As part of a low income family, no way could I have afforded fees to go on a
Second Chance course. Besides, my self importance rated me barely visible –
to spend money on such a luxury as education for me was unthinkable,
especially when food, clothes and children's shoes was a pressing reality.

In the present economic climate the struggle to preserve good childcare and cheap
and free courses is enormous. Like many other women's groups we've seen these
resources cut back to the bone in recent years by those who provide our funds. But
the issue is not just to do with money and the derisory amounts of financial support
given to women – it is also concerned with political priorities. In a society which
pays lip service to equal opportunities and women's rights, we find our rights and
opportunities continually under attack. The backlash against women in the present
political climate, and the ways in which this affects our education, is something we'll
return to in the next chapter. First we need to remind ourselves of what is at stake.

For many adult education may be viewed as a 'pastime', a 'non-essential', a
'frill'. Something to fill in the time during winter evenings or when 'too much leisure'
becomes a problem. In some circles – as we've seen – education for women has
become the latest of many professional bandwagons. This is not our view. For most of
us – with few resources to call our own and little enough power in the world – we
think of education as a tool. Something to help us change our lives and help re-create
the world in a different way. Not just by getting qualifications or even a well-paid job
– although both of these are useful assets which most of us don't already have – but as
a way to challenge the present order of things. The sort of women's education we
have in mind is an education controlled by women for women. It means taking
resources usually monopolised by men away from men and concentrating them in
the hands of women. It means learning together effective ways in which we can
challenge patriarchy in our everyday lives for the benefit of ourselves and for women
generally. Women's education, as we define it, is political education linked to women's
liberation.

Considerable numbers of education courses aimed at women aren't of course
based on this assumption, especially when their organisers have patronising ideas
about the limitations of our expectations, or thinly disguised male views of scholarship and excellence. But courses that are set up by women, with feminist intent, and
which place commitment to women's lives and struggles before any other consideration, are likely, by the very nature of their women-positive, pro-women character, to

be concerned with social change and liberation. Sometimes, even when they're not, the experience of being with other women, and in the company of feminist ideas, can trigger lift off.

> *I'm not sure what attracted me to the Changing Experience of Women course. I'd been studying with the Open University for years, and this was the last half credit to get an Honours degree. During my studies I'd become a Marxist. I was active in CND (Campaign for Nuclear Disarmament), a steward at work for Nalgo (National Association of Local Government Officers), working with unemployed kids on YTS (Youth Training Scheme) etc. I was divorced, living contentedly alone. Feminism was something I'd heard of vaguely, and seemed trivial and dull. The course wasn't much different from any other OU course that I'd done. So I thought. But then came THE SUMMER SCHOOL. This included analysis of ordinary cinema film, a workshop to design a sex education course for school children, and a workshop of role-playing a Trade Union dispute with male managers and male union officials (role-played by women) representing the aggrieved women's workforce. And much more. In particular, the summer school was almost completely women only. No group had to have one of the 2 or 3 male oddities in with them if they didn't want to. I opted for women-only groups throughout. And there was a women only disco one evening – the first disco I ever enjoyed in my life! The freedom to **dance.** I know this was a 'turning point'. The **experience of** the Women's Studies one week school was such that 'nothing would ever be the same again'! I noticed, when revising for the exam at the end of the year, that my pre-summer school essays with their Marxist line seemed, well, dull and trivial. Within a year of finishing Changing Experience of Women I had left my 'straight job' (no more straight high income), sold my house, got a job in a workers co-op and changed my surname. I cannot seem to find the commitment I used to have to working for change within the organisations (patriarchal) that I used to care about. Changing Experience of Women was the only bit of my whole education that I **lived**, rather than just read up.*

When courses are more explicitly committed to black and working class women, to our increasing independence, our economic advancement and our growing self-esteem, we know that we're into something pretty remarkable.

> *I knew as soon as I had those pipes in my hand that I wanted to be a plumber. I don't know why, I just knew that I couldn't get enough of this. I wanted to learn all I could. I was amazed at how easy it was. I was always led to believe that the tools were dangerous, but here I was using them. Things that I had been told I would never be able to understand, I could.*

> *The Women's Training Scheme has given me a lot more than just skills in Auto Engineering. It has given me confidence, staying power, opportunities, support and friendship. And the will to support other women who want to go into male dominated skill areas. And pride when I realise there are things I*

can do. *Things are not as difficult or alien for us as men would have us believe.*

I can't begin to explain how much it meant to me, but I do know that because of the course my life has been enriched beyond measure; it has virtually meant a new life for me.

Some of us got involved in women's education at critical times in our lives when we were in danger of going under.

It was the best thing that happened to me at one of the worst times of my life, and without it I feel I could have gone to pieces. Sharing experiences with other women has been very supportive. It's helped me regain a perspective and the hope that life still has a lot to offer.

I felt I had wasted so many years. Where had I been, what had I been doing all this time? It seemed really urgent to regain myself before it was too late, to do something worthwhile and interesting. After being silenced for so long it was difficult to feel confidence in my own voice. But I was freed from silent life where my thoughts and needs could never be fully expressed because no-one had really listened or cared. I had become a slave of my own oppression: always giving in, compromising my true beliefs to gain nothing, always trying to please everyone else but never myself. Thinking I could not survive on my own, dependent on those who gave me very little in return. What was I? What had I been? Someone's daughter, girlfriend, lover, wife, mother. My needs and ambitions never really being fulfilled, an identity that belonged to others. I had been servile, hidden, put down. Always conforming to please others to gain affection and love that was in reality empty of loyalty and depth.

I was at a crossroads in my life after having been married for 22 years and having brought up my children. All this seemed to end when my marriage was ended by my husband walking out of my life for good. He had left me. I didn't know any other life. I was left empty, nothing in my life to do and no proper qualifications. I am broken hearted about my marriage ending, but I knew I had to start a new life somehow. That's when I started Second Chance.

It's not unusual for women to feel insignificant and marginal. It's very clear where the power lies in our society and what little importance is attached to the quality of women's lives. Poverty, racism and women-hating are effective controls on any sense of pride, confidence or ambition.

My life seems to have been mapped out for me in this dependent role. I wish it had been different – that I had been given alternatives to learn from, to aim for, giving me a choice that would make me financially secure, so that I could have then decided on equal terms if I wanted a man to share my life.

Of course quite a lot more has to change before patriarchy takes a topple – but the more we pick away at its foundations, and reclaim some control over our own affairs, the less dutiful and the more independent we become.

I have benefitted by having a chance to discuss my ideas with other women and to realise how much we have in common – so many of us have doubts about ourselves, about why we have certain things or why we feel certain ways. This discussion gives you confidence and support. You no longer feel isolated and this leads you to start looking for answers, not just for yourself but for women in general.

Before this course I felt like I was in a cocoon, unable to break out. Since starting I have broken out and am just spreading my wings. My colours are starting to show through. I know that by the end of it I will have learnt to fly.

This course should be the right of all women, not only for the skills but also for the confidence and self-esteem. It's an awakening.

Being on Second Chance has made me revalue myself. A school failure perhaps – but why should I take all the blame? I didn't fail the system, it failed me. Second Chance has given me confidence, and like a candle I burn brighter when I'm with other women who are the same. It's much harder and exhausting now – the same flame is flickering when placed in the everyday hassle of life, but I still burn. I'm not putting myself down. I don't want to lose the truth I've found or the confidence of my own worth.

I began to liken myself to the last onion in the vegetable rack, the one we get so familiar with we don't notice until it gets beyond use; the one that when we finally start to peel off layers of skin, emerges as a bright and firm and very usable onion after all.

Whatever images we use to describe our 'emergence' as bright and useful onions, 'flickering flames' or 'spectacular butterflies', increasing self-esteem, a new sense of purpose and rekindled courage are common responses to feminist education.

All my life I've always taken second best, but I know now what I want to do and be and no-one is going to stop me. Let them try and I might go down, but I will go down fighting. Then I might just surprise them and get up again. Just because I'm a woman, they can't say no.

And it's not only because we feel inspired by the promise of new, skills or a job, but also because we are relieved to have our significance confirmed.

Qualifications nil – straight into a factory, that's ME. It took Second Chance to assure me that what was pressed between my two ears was a person, and that what I had to say was important.

One of the major achievements of patriarchy is to fill us full of doubts about our own worth. Anti-woman propaganda and misogynist information on a massive scale can, as we have seen in earlier chapters, make us feel useless and even responsible for our own predicaments. Those of us who feel angry, restless or rebellious about the extremely little lot usually reserved for women get maligned as 'difficult' or 'embittered'. Those of us who get smashed by poverty, violence or hatred get defined as 'mad'. It is highly empowering to discover in discussion with other women that as individuals we are far from unique in our reactions to poverty, powerless and isolation. To want more out of life is not a personal deficiency or a minor insanity. The appropriate response is not to feel guilty. We are not victims of our own inadequacy. Quite the reverse. When we start looking outside ourselves for explanations that make sense of our lives, male power and women's oppression are quite clearly related.

When I started Second Chance I was feeling resentful and bitter about my inability to change my relationship with my husband and improve things for my family. But now I feel less dependent on him for approval or decision making, and am learning to feel better about myself as an independent woman with my own needs. I like to think that I no longer care what my husband thinks about me. I have been using him as a measuring stick for my success or failure for too long – now I shall start using my own standards. I think it is possible for me to be myself, as well as a wife and mother. I feel more optimistic about my own future now and more determined than ever to do some of those things I have always wanted to do.

Until I became involved in feminist education there were whole areas of my life that I never spoke about to anyone: experiences from way back that I never been able to discuss, and least of all with the people I was supposed to be close to, like my husband, my family.

Some women on the course said that it took them a long time to feel safe to talk about certain things, but to be honest I was so amazed that anyone wanted to know about the skeletons in my cupboard I didn't stop to think – I just couldn't believe that the deep, dark secrets I'd been hiding for so long had happened to other women too. Like feeling angry and resentful towards. my son, feeling trapped and out of control of my life. The panic attacks, feeling strange about going out sometimes. having been beaten up by a boyfriend, and feeling ashamed, thinking it was my fault, actually allowing myself to be persuaded that the beatings were proof that he cared about me. It's hard to describe the relief in discovering that you really aren't mad, that if the world feels strange it's because it is strange and distorted, not your fault at all, and that there are actually words to describe all of that which makes perfect sense to a whole lot of other women,

We also know that feelings of personal failure aren't confined to black and working-class women.

Before undertaking the course I thought I knew exactly where I was in society and what the future held for me. I had been brought up to believe that a 'good wife' kept the home clean, did the washing and ironing, shopped for, prepared and cooked the food and, most importantly, was always smartly dressed for her husband. The cardinal sin for my generation (born 1939) was the wife who had 'let herself go'. Where she had gone no-one was sure, but in ceasing to care for her appearance, she had ceased to be of value. She was an abject failure. In my professional life (upon whose scene I was a very late arrival) I have doubted my own capabilities (despite obtaining a good degree) and, if I am honest, I have always deferred to the opinion of men. Now, seventeen months into this course, I feel that I have been the subject of

*massive brainwashing for the past 47 years, and have been coerced into a
role which I no longer feel can accommodate my needs. I feel a growing
sense of awareness and my confidence and competence are developing daily.*

'Developing awareness', 'competence' and 'confidence' are all experiences that we
can relate to. Whereas our other experiences of 'education' contributed to putting us
down and keeping us in our place, learning together with other women in the spirit
of feminist education produces a quite different effect.

*There was a sense of belonging with other women – women who felt the
same commitment to a cause that cares about women, our rights to equality
and independence and the struggle for power. Usually my mind was spinning
with emotions when I got home: anger and sadness because of women's
oppression and the violence we suffer; enthusiasm and hope for the future
projects and campaigns; affections and togetherness for the women who care
and those who had become my friends. Emotions which had lain dormant
except as a servant of others were now **my** emotions, sharing needs, hopes,
dreams. I felt on a sort of 'high' a lot of the time. I felt elated, happy,
inspired, useful – felt I could take on anything and win. It set me on the path
to regaining my identity.*

*Before I went on Second Chance my life was one big boring existence.
Tuesdays used to be one of the days I went to a centre for the disabled,
where I was expected to make baskets or stools or do knitting. My life was
going too quickly, and yet too slowly. I had to do something else. Second
Chance is doing for me exactly what the title says. It's certainly given me the
chance to learn that I am not a freak or abnormal. I'm just another woman,
as normal in the head as the next. It sounds crazy, but if I wasn't sitting in
this wheelchair I think I'd have quite forgotten, now that I am different. I've
always hated asking for help but sometimes I have to, but most women on
Second Chance know I need help with the toilet, so I'm no longer
embarrassed to ask. I now don't feel anywhere near as chair-conscious as I
used to, thanks to the support I've gained here.*

*I felt very nervous to begin with, it felt like going into the unknown, I've
never done anything like this before. When I was married I was at home all
day doing housework, then a cleaning job, in the evenings, but my job came
to an end when my husband left so all I had was the housework. By going on
Second Chance it was a challenge to me, to save my self respect and
confidence and, most of all, to learn more so I could in future be able to get
a job. At first I found it very difficult to concentrate, but I began to feel
more at home when we began to share our own personal experiences. Then I
was able to settle down to do the work because I had support and
understanding from the rest of the women and also the tutors. They all
became my friends, which I've never had before. They are helping me get
through a very bad time of my life. So I coped with the work involved on the
course. I haven't before done any sort of writing, only Christmas and
birthday cards, so I never even wrote letters. But I felt so relaxed on Second*

*Chance and look forward to every Thursday when I could go again and see
my new made friends. I was now able to study and I began to see things
differently, and I had no problems about coming here, no matter how bad I
felt inside. I was beginning to think for myself, not feeling just a machine. I
am feeling better about myself because I'm using my brain. Second Chance
has given me an education which I want, to go into life with hope of a better
job – one which I can call a career as well and also to go on with life, coping
with my problems, with the support of all my new friends. It has given me
the will to get on with my own life instead of thinking to end it, which I
thought many times before coming here.*

There is a moment in the experience of women's education at its best – which in
different ways, at different times, for different women – allows 'the blinkers to come
off', 'the penny to drop' and 'the light to dawn'. It's an experience which we often
hear women refer to. From the point at which we realise that our dissatisfactions are
not unreasonable, our anger is justified, and our problems are political, we have the
makings of a whole new perspective on the world. And whatever the discussion, the
emotion or the personal association is which brings us to that point of recognition –
of ceasing to blame ourselves and beginning to recognise the power of patriarchy for
what it is – we know that, inside our heads at least, nothing will ever be quite the
same again. From that moment – to use a well-known feminist cliche – there's no
turning back. And these are moments which come not from the 'influence of extremists' but from the piecing together the truth about our lives in serious debate with
other women. It can be a passionate and emotional experience. It's the kind of passion which leads to making monumental changes and to questioning old loyalties.

*I like being in a women-only group that's feeling emotional or passionate or
angry about something. The careful, engrossed attention from those listening,
with contributions bursting out of an exacting concern to reveal the
complexity of truth and emotion and meaning – testimonies of women –
anecdotes to validate insights and experiences across different barriers of age
and 'race' and background. Spontaneous irreverence and jokes, and bodies
registering courage, resistance, strength. The woman who makes us laugh or
cry or bleed, or who gets up 'to do the actions' she is describing. The woman
who says 'Yes, that's right, that's how I feel too'. In those women's groups I
have felt love for women and pride and delight in women. I've hugged
women I'd never met before and I've felt close to women in ways that men
could never make me feel. When I listen to what some men do to women I
find it hard to like them anymore.*

Which is not to suggest that 'old loyalties' don't die hard. As working class women
we'd be naive to forget the ways in which the middle class organise society for their
own benefit, and that middle class men don't need to worry as long as middle class
women like Margaret Thatcher are taking care of their interests.

*God knows we can understand
your thrifty little ways
brought up to slice the bacon thin*

and save for better days.
But some of us are wondering now
what else you've got in mind.
You want the fat, you want the lean,
you even want the rind.
And God knows we can understand
the business of the scales,
brought up to weigh the basic needs
and she that loses fails.
But some of us are thinking now
about those weights you use.
We think you've hung them round our necks
and that is why we lose.
And God knows we can understand
why you're still selling things,
brought up to mind the counter
and not to pull the strings.
But some of us are tired now
so when you say your prayers
could you tell the big inspector
that we're after even shares.

As lesbians we know that ignorance and prejudice still come from women who have chosen to believe men's lies about us. Or women who are so used to thinking in heterosexist ways that we remain invisible.

I spent 2 years doing a diploma in Women's Studies – the only lesbian in the group so far as I know – although some women dropped out and talking about your personal experience wasn't encouraged. Only two sessions in two years focussed on lesbian issues. I felt completely invisible in that group and was reduced to silence – even during the two sessions they decided to discuss me.

Ignoring lesbian existence and making heterosexuality 'the norm' is a common occurrence. But while ignorance is bad enough, prejudice and hatred are even worse.

I remember co-leading a discussion about 'loving women' to which enormous numbers of ostensibly 'straight' women turned up. It always amazes me how popular such discussions turn out to be among women who 'are not lesbian but . . .' and who often look more like dykes than dykes. However . . . we were talking about the ways in which lesbians are stigmatised in ways that, as well as being personally damaging, are also used against us in custody battles and in debarring us from jobs. In the event we didn't need to 'import' illustrations of what we meant into the group. One woman said she'd never allow lesbians or gays to baby sit for her children just in case . . . Another – waxing to her theme of insatiable promiscuity – said she knew about lesbians, 'they did it like dogs on the carpet'.

A commitment to feminism doesn't automatically eradicate racism, as many black feminists have discovered to their cost.

> I went to the meeting to talk about 'feminism'. By the time I got there – 14 miles on public transport – I was late. I was the only one who in their eyes didn't 'measure up' to the group. I understand perfectly what they were on about but what's different about me is that I don't look like them, or dress like them, or live like them, and by making the effort to go to the meeting, I have spent money that I can ill afford. I think they like to think of themselves as 'liberal feminists' – they're all white, they've got good jobs, comfortable homes, husbands. If this was to happen to me a year ago it would put me off feminism for good. They would have depressed me down to the ground. Women like this used to be able to do this to me the same as men.

With old loyalties still intact and old contradictions still in evidence, we have considerable work still to do in resolving the conflicts we have inherited from men.

> Not all women in groups feel so good. There are differences between us which we didn't create, but which we've inherited from men, and which still conspire to divide us. I think we should be angry with each other and certainly we should he critical of each other. But when we can't talk to each other anymore, then we're doing men's work for them. We can say the differences don't matter – in a weedy liberal kind of way – or retreat into therapy or meditation as an easier option. We can say that it's all too painful and turn our anger inwards, or our feelings of betrayal onto each other. But then nothing will change. Patriarchy will win so long as we help to keep alive the hatred men have created and the systems of oppression that go with it. Women's groups **don't** feel so good to me when we can't see the wood for trees and when its men who get in our way.

Preventing men from 'getting in the way' is, of course, much easier said than done. Two thousand years plus of patriarchal power won't shrivel up and go away because some of us have decided to give priority to ourselves and other women rather than to men. But reclaiming our self-esteem and taking more control over our lives is not a bad place to start.

At the Women's Education Centre in Southampton the struggle to establish, and hold on to, a small, under-funded and borrowed space for women has been enormous. Funding bodies have been critical of our feminist politics and women-only provision. Traditionally-minded sponsors of some of our courses – the university extra-mural department, and the local authority – have exercised continuing interference in our work which has been at best unhelpful and at worst utterly destructive. It is some tribute to the persistence and courage of women over the years that, despite an increasingly hostile backlash to feminism generally in society, and a specifically localised attack on our existence, we continue to survive. But more of this in the next chapter.

The hostility to women-centred education from anti-feminist forces of one kind or another does not detract from the benefits we know we have gained from what we have achieved together. No doubt 'the powers that be' would have given us an easier time if we had agreed to compromise, let men take part in what we do and exert their influence over our decisions. But then, we'd have been back into the usual business of learning altogether different lessons about the world – lessons which wouldn't have been concerned with women's liberation. Arguments for women-only classes are sometimes presented as remedial provision, as though we need to 'cling together' and 'build up our self-confidence' in a 'sheltered environment 'away from the 'rough and tumble of everyday life'. As those well used to the rough and tumble of the real world know – it's not self-confidence we need, but power.

We don't exclude men from what we do because we're 'practising' so that we can 'cope better' when it comes to the 'real thing', or men's education, later on. We're involved in making our own separate and different education tradition. We don't include men because we have our own history and culture to reclaim, our own knowledge to create, our own skills to identify and use and our own political priorities to attend to. We're not concerned about 'copying men' or 'seeking their approval', we're concerned with making our own freedom. And this means refusing to be diverted by the usual submissions which are made on their behalf.

> As far as I'm concerned, words are cheap. Men can and do say all sorts of things but never mean them. If a man wants me to believe he's trying to be non-sexist then he's got to show it – he's got to **live it** – not just keep telling me. I may want to believe him – but I won't trust him. The fact is, although a particular man may not personally harass or intimidate or abuse women, that is a **choice** – he has chosen not to act in the approved male way. But he could change his mind at any time, and he knows it. And, according to the sanctioned power over women he has by virtue of being male, he will get away with it.

Others, we are told, will improve with education.

> I get really pissed off hearing the same old thing – 'Why don't you let men in, they need education as well?' Well, I'm sick of being expected to do everything for men. If they want to know why we're so angry, if they **really** care about the way things are in this sick world of theirs, then that's fine, I'm all for that. But they've got to go and sort it out themselves – get together with other men and tackle their own sexism and behaviour – not expect us to tell them yet again. Women have spent hundreds of years telling men that the problem is them – and what they should do about it, but they don't really want to know. They pretend. They pay lip service to women's rights, but at heart they don't want to, and won't give up their power. The quicker we realise that what they're most dead keen on is keeping the differences and inequalities between us, the less time we'll have to spend wasting our breath explaining and negotiating with them.

Often, it is claimed, men's support will give us more credibility, but

> We don't want men here to give it bogus 'status' or respectability. We don't need it. Women's Education is the most important activity that we have

engaged in in our lives; it already has the highest possible status in our eyes, and we don't care what men think of it.

Although not all of us agree that men are 'the enemy', we do agree that they don't contribute very much to making things any better.

After a lifetime of listening to them droning on about football, sex, real ale and politics in that order, I just know what it could be like having men in our group. Reducing our urgent and desperate questioning to 'why don't we want doors opened for us anymore'! Most of us don't give a shit about doors being opened for us, unless when we pass through, there is financial independence and the freedom to live our lives as we choose, waiting on the other side. Most doors have 'Keep Out' stamped on them, and it's only men who can open them.

Doing it all ourselves is of course very threatening to men. Who knows where such behaviour will lead? Keep fit classes and jumble sales are one thing, but becoming a plumber or going to Greenham suggests defiance, moving in and taking over – an altogether different challenge to men's authority.

Men don't want to concern themselves with the separate worlds we live in – we can spend most of our time with other women, just so long as we never forget that our role is really all about looking after and servicing men. We can join cookery classes with other women or slimming clubs with other women, or go to Tupperware parties or Mother and Toddler groups because they are 'safe' activities – safe for men. They make no challenge to our role as wife and mother and housekeeper. But most of all, they present no threat to male power. Involvement in Women's Education, however, is a threat to men's power – and they know it. Witness their panicked and desperate tactics to try and stop us: the image of the fat, ugly, loony feminist; the guilt they load on us about 'neglecting' our children; 'experts' (men) telling us how we will 'lose' our femininity; and their distortion of women loving and caring about each other revealed in their hate-filled and offensive insults about lesbians.

Seen from our point of view, of course, the absence of men is the very ingredient that makes the experience of women's education empowering.

I'm no longer invisible. Now I can challenge what people say, I can speak my mind and feel confident I was never specifically taught these skills – we didn't sit down and actually learn how to be confident, or how to question things or express our opinions. This process came about through doing courses with women where we worked collectively, learning from each other, and where there was an atmosphere that gave us freedom of voice. Ideas were created, old memories were reborn. We were on the same wavelength. Irreverent jokes sparked off spontaneous laughter, important insights received validation. We listened to each other and we all cared if someone was going through a problem, or we all rejoiced when someone took another step *towards her liberation. The only place where this can be achieved is in feminist, women-only courses, because then the knowledge we need and want is **ours** and is relevant to our lives as women. We need to be on our own because, as one of our sisters frequently reminds us, 'you don't plan the jailbreak with the screws in the room'.*

*After years of self-denial, losing confidence and any sense of self worth, I'm at last feeling I am important, My reasons for not looking out for myself, for not thinking about what I wanted or needed, fitted neatly into the mould expected in a patriarchal family. I was aware that I might be at odds with all that and feel guilty – now I **know** I'm at odds with it and I'm **enjoying** it.*

Two ingredients are important in the curriculum of women's education. One is that the content should be women-centred – about women's lives, about the world seen through women's eyes, about issues, skills and information likely to increase women's independence and choice. Knowledge, attitudes and assumptions about women which are intended to restrict our independence, misconstrue our past and mislead our futures are not in our best interests and have no place in the curriculum of women's studies. The other ingredient is relevance. Relevance not to the limitations and restrictions which are currently imposed upon us by domesticity and powerlessness, but relevance to what we need to know and what we need to do to transform our lives.

Whilst many different women would make all kinds of claims for including different information, ideas and skills in women's education, the test of their relevance is as much to do with intention as content. The purpose in feminist education is concerned with our liberation and independence, and with learning politically and socially useful knowledge in a positive and encouraging atmosphere. Too often, as we've already seen, courses aimed at women are deliberately arranged to avoid contention. Those who want to educate us think that, as working-class women, we'll be afraid or put off by any suggestion of feminism. So we get offered things like keep fit and machine knitting. Although many of us writing this book wouldn't have called ourselves feminists when we got involved in women's education, we knew there was plenty that was wrong with our lives, and that what we wanted was dramatic changes. Now, being feminist means we're actively involved in making them. It's much less contentious, of course, to keep looking for problems within yourself than start making the connections between male power and women's oppression. And some varieties of women's education are in danger of preserving such delusions. Assertiveness training, for example.

I think for many of us, assertiveness training seems to be a logical step in trying to find ways of dealing with the world that don't leave us feeling more powerless and frustrated. I suppose that we all, at some time in our struggles, cling on to the naive belief that if only we ask in the proper way, express our needs and wants clearly enough, be assertive enough, we might get our fair share of the world. Naive it certainly is. You only have to look at some of the mass of current literature, aimed at helping women to be more assertive, like A Woman In Your Own Right by Anne Dickson, for

*example. I would have to say that the central struggles of my existence, and
of the women I see around me, do not consist of getting waiters to notice me
in a restaurant, returning a steak that is not cooked properly or holding out
for the best apples in the greengrocer's pile. I suspect that I could role play
these situations until I get an Oscar, but I would, like most women, still be
denied the right to a decent job, a decent standard of living for me and my
kid, and still be unable to walk about the streets alone and unmolested. And
if I ever get closer to a steak than gazing at it in a butcher's window, on my
way to buy the sausages, I wouldn't give a bugger how it was cooked. I take
issue with Ms. Dickson when she suggests I argue my way out of sexual
harassment with the cool logic of her assertive techniques. Suggesting that
women can talk themselves out of being raped is as bad as men telling us we
provoke them. The logic of both arguments is that sexual harassment and
rape are our own fault – the new twist in the tale presumably being that
these won't happen to us if we are only assertive enough. A great many
women could testify that men will persist a great deal more strongly than this
– they will threaten and use fists or knives or bottles, and will claim
afterwards that 'No', no matter how assertively we learn to say it, really still
meant 'Yes'. Are our problems as women really caused by not being assertive
enough? Certainly we are conditioned to put our own needs last, but we also
have to acknowledge that men have the power to make sure women's needs
continue to be ignored. Seeing ourselves as deficient in life's little 'Social
Skills' isn't really going to change that.*

Neither is the concentration on the kind of games and exercises which seem increasingly popular in some Women's Studies courses.

*I feel as if in my search for answers to serious questions about my life, I've
wasted an awful lot of time playing silly-bugger games. After half a lifetime
of being put down, trivialised, mocked and treated with contempt by men, I
can't believe some of the games I've been willing to put myself through
thinking I might learn something. Trust games where you lean on each other,
games where you close your eyes and wander around encountering bodies,
games where you draw pictures of yourself as you'd like to be (particularly
humiliating as I never could get any further than stick people). Games where
you hop around the room looking for symbiosis or wear a drawing around
your neck. I'm not saying some of it isn't fun, but what does it achieve? If
fun is the object I'd rather spend my money in the pub. Doing unthreatening
things like trust games in the company of lots of nice women can feel safe,
make me feel good, but I think I've learned more and achieved more when
I've been angry and upset at what men do to us.*

The lurch towards counselling and therapy models in women's education, apart from
being thoroughly middle class in inspiration, is also politically dangerous for women.
The problem with all of these approaches is that they all sidestep the real issues of
male power and control. They don't attack the structures of dominance that are used

by men to keep us in our defined place. They don't confront male power or attempt radical social change, which is what is needed to improve our lives as women. We need our anger. It can be creative. We must not allow it to be dissipated. We don't need it to be 'smoothed away' by meditation, or to be transferred on to a white-coated 'expert', or for it to be managed away through therapy. We need our anger to galvanise us to work and fight together.

Take psychotherapy, for example – from where a lot of these developments in women's education have their origins – and which also encourages another model of 'white-coated expert'. In a world of 'caring and sharing' and 'working on' your problems, the reverence given to co-counselling adds to the deception of equality. Just as those who are being paid as counsellors to listen and cuddle and question do not reveal their own vulnerabilities and anxieties to those they regard as 'clients', neither do women's studies tutors 'experienced in group work' forget the importance of their own detachment. It may be explained as 'protecting students from becoming too dependent' or 'enabling students to arrive at their own solutions' or preventing tutors from being questioned in ways that stop students from 'facing up to their own problems'. But all of these are ways of rationalising a distance which is based on the assumption that tutors and students are somehow different. Although the atmosphere is often caring and the language is kindly, the underlying assumptions are nonetheless those of 'experts' and 'others'; of 'us' and 'them'.

One of the criticisms we have made of men's education is its hierarchical and competitive approach to learning as the reflection of male power structures in the wider society. We have also seen how academic feminism is in danger of repeating the same patterns because of the concern to establish some kind of respectability for feminism. 'Therapeutic' approaches to women's education may appear to be more democratic, but are actually dependent on tutors not getting 'too emotionally involved' with their students, rather like conscientious social workers. This is not the kind of relationship on which women's equality and liberation will be based.

In the Women's Liberation Movement here has always been a suspicion of experts, hierarchies and leaders, because all of them prevent us speaking for ourselves, taking control of our own lives and finding better, less divisive and oppressive ways of organising ourselves and living together. We think that in women's education the emphasis should be on learning from each other, on making sense of our own and other women's personal experience, and making theories together which do justice to the complexity and difference of our lives. Tutors might have skills that we can learn from – like electrical engineering or computer programming – but they have no business to set themselves apart as some kind of role model. Neither should we forget that we also have skills that are just as valuable. In this sense we are all teachers and we are all learners.

If we have been persuaded to believe in our own ignorance by the oppressive messages of our early education and our everyday lives, we have to begin revaluing ourselves and reclaiming our lives in the company of others we do regard as our equals. We also have to expect that such a transformation of what is usually regarded as education may take a little while to get used to! At its best it will be a mixture of intellectual, emotional and political intensity, so that nothing will ever seem quite the same again.

> I am not enjoying the course. I go along every Tuesday, quite happy in my mindless, self-denial world, only to be slowly woken during the hours of the day. Suddenly I find that somehow the sincerity of the women around me makes me feel safe – that it's alright to talk of those inner-most pains and fears and no-one will say those dreaded words 'Oh stop being a martyr. Pull yourself together.' The women there listen with intensity of genuine concern, companionship, empathy. That's it, we have empathy for each other. Because of that we really talk to one another. It is **wonderful**. Real people talking about real happenings, important issues and maybe affecting each other's lives, not only by removing communicative barriers, but also within ourselves. I for one have dared to confess to myself some of the thoughts that I would not listen to. Those thoughts that hurt right into the depths of my soul. Not only did I stop and listen, but I spoke of them as well! Everyone listened, no-one told me off for dramatics. I showed my real self and I was accepted. Oh, the elation. I feel supported, cared about, and glad that people know I need to be hugged. Sometimes a hug can hold a person together. In a friend's arms I feel safe and if someone cares about me enough to hold me whilst I crawl out of my head, then what a **great** friend I have. But no, despite this, I can't say I enjoy the course. It makes me think so hard and so deeply, I have to start facing up to the fact that if I'm not to blame, someone or something out there has got it in for women. It's no longer possible to keep believing the usual old lies. When I go home I am drained, emotionally washed out, intellectually exhausted – almost glad it's over. I will tell you this though. Through the tiredness I do feel that was a day well spent. I have learned more about society, more about my friends and more about me. It is challenging but satisfying, frightening and enlightening, intrusive but awakening, frustrating but hopeful, annoying but calming. And a great many more mixed emotions. So all in all it's probably one of the best things that I have ever done with my life.

At its best it will help make a 'reclaimed identity' into a whole new identity.

> At 28 years old, I thought that the best job I could get if I was lucky would be in a shop or a factory. Then I got a chance to go to college via the Nottingham Women's Training Scheme, and I have never looked back. I chose to do Electrical Engineering, something I never would have seen myself doing – until I got this chance. Naturally, I've had some snide remarks about me wanting to do 'a man's job', but I don't see why I, or any other woman, should only be thought suitable to be cleaners, dinner ladies or typists. Even if a man has the same job as a woman, the title is different. A man is a chef, whereas a woman is a cook. The word chef stands out to be important – a cook doesn't. Who is to say that electricians, plumbers, mechanics and lorry drivers have to be men? – I can't see why women should be thought

incapable of being anything they want to be. Going back to learning is the best thing I've done for a long time and I'd recommend it to any woman – no matter what subject she is interested in.

At its best it will provide inspiration and the courage to make difficult political choices.

When I listened to the Latin American women – who are political refugees in Britain – talking about revolution and machismo, I felt utterly inspired by their strength and their conviction. The Women's Liberation Movement feels extremely timid here at times, and whilst we can explain all this as an exhaustion born of fighting anti-feminism and the massive social and political backlash against women, nothing could be more crippling than the conditions of women in El Salvador, Chile and Guatemala. Talking with the Latin American women made me feel even more impatient with the complacency and liberalism of some British feminism – the naivety with which we put faith in attitudinal solutions rather than face up to the implications of gross inequalities of wealth and power and resources, the reluctance to hear what working class and black women are saying about class and racism and the attempt to keep lesbian women quiet in case we give the Movement a bad name.

The Latin American women were quite unequivocal. Social change for women needs to be both a political and economic revolution as well as a cultural revolution. Men may not be the enemy but they have to stop acting as the oppressors. When I think of the tangles some British feminists get into to avoid the truth about all of this and the continual 'benefit of the doubt' we somehow manage to sustain in the face of gross male violence, enormous poverty and widespread racism, it makes me very angry at our prevarication and retreat.

What makes feminist education special is that we're making women-centred knowledge in collective ways. We're linking together personal experience, powerful ideas, strong emotions and political action on our own behalf, in a way that makes education not just about being clever and getting qualifications but about changing the world for women. It's not only what we learn that matters, it's **how** we learn that's important, and in both of these respects we have to be in control of what we do. The overriding power and potential for interference from men will never be far away. We have no illusions about the patriarchal world in which we're trying to build some space, but we also know that, in the end, 'doing it for ourselves' is the only way in which we'll ever change that world.

It's not role models we require – successful women doing men's jobs and beating the boys at their own games – but a vision that includes greater freedom for us all. At a time when popular pundits are already proclaiming the Women's Movement dead and feminism defeated, it feels more important than ever to hold on to the truth of what we know about what we need and what we want for the future.

Learning, liberation and maturity: an open letter to whoever's left

(Originally published in *Adults Learning*, Vol 4, no 9, May 1993)

After an absence of some four years from teaching and writing in adult education and at the point when fourteen years of New Right thinking in education had effectively changed the agenda of adult learning in Britain (closely to be followed by Australia and New Zealand) Thompson returned to the debate with an open letter in **Adults Learning** *which provoked a deluge of letters in response – the majority, but not all of them, in broad agreement. She identifies the ways in which priorities had shifted, creating a completely different culture and purpose in mainstream provision; whilst complacency regarding structural inequalities, including a strong backlash against political education and feminism, had intensified. Writing in 1993 she was reasonably accurate about the extent to which the glory, glory days of Thatcherism, as manifested in the Conservative Party were numbered, presenting the Left and the labour movement generally with fresh opportunities to reclaim the radical initiative. Writing now in 1997 she probably sees Blair more as the 'natural heir' to Thatcherism than the principled defender of socialist and collective values against the individualising and moralistic posturing of corporate politics.*

Learning, liberation and maturity: an open letter to whoever's left

Forgive me if what follows lacks the usual scholarly rigour associated with contributions to this journal. But I need to know if there's anyone out there who cares very much any more about the radical tradition in adult education.

Back in the 'good old days' when some of us who talked about structural inequality, institutional racism and gendered power relations, were considered 'dangerously extreme' by the liberal establishment and caricatured by some as 'the young turks', it was at least possible to discuss politics.

Oppression and the class struggle, patriarchy and feminism, cultural imperialism and endemic racism were not everyday debates within the liberal tradition – but there was sufficient space around the edges from which to be subversive and within which to keep alive the visions and ideals of independent working class education that we inherited from the beginning of the labour and trade union movements, and from the activity of working class feminists at the turn of the century.

I suppose we were all children of the sixties who had sharpened our appetite for social change on the urgency and aspirations of the New Left and in the resurgence of the Women's Movement. We applied our Marxist, socialist and feminist understanding of the world to our practice as teachers, finding inspiration in theories concerned with 'really useful knowledge', praxis, conscientisation and critical intelligence. We were concerned to make links between the social and material conditions of oppression and the possibility of education as a tool in the pursuit of personal and collective liberation.

Adult education that expressed itself 'in solidarity' with working class, black and women's struggles was, of course, always a minority pursuit. We exaggerated, in retrospect, the treachery of liberal complacency and wasted too much energy on the intensity of short term initiatives. Just at the moment when, waiting in the wings, a much more serious challenge was gaining ground.

Like others on the Left, we underestimated the relentless, ruthless and amoral quality of Thatcherism, as we observed the world shift before our eyes and found, as we floundered, the language of liberalism and radicalism re-appropriated into the vocabulary of the re-invigorated Right. The rest is history.

Now, thirteen years on from *Adult Education for a Change* and ten years after *Learning Liberation* I return to the frontline much like a dinosaur. To find the literature of journals and the rationale of conferences preoccupied with the management of the education marketplace. In which the talk is about strategic plans and targeting techniques, about franchising and credit transfers, about twilight shifts and accelerated degrees – delivered with the kind of tenacity devoid of passion that characterises automatons released from business training schemes.

The discussion is all about institutional adjustments and market forces, in which students have become another niche market in the post Fordist vision of flexible specialisation. In which big and powerful institutions sub-contract less prestigious work to small and struggling institutions. And in which grey men in suits, with executive briefcases and brightly coloured ties, skilled in business speak, manage the decisions that deliver fresh batches of new consumers in search of educational commodities into lecture halls and classrooms, staffed at the chalk face by contract labour whose terms and conditions of employment have been so deregulated as to ensure maximum exploitation at minimum cost.

And what of adult students? What experience – transformational or otherwise – might they expect to derive from being packed into the academic confines of former polytechnics? Or shunted through increasingly more complex regulations and towards increasingly more tenacious hurdles as the business of Access and APEL becomes the latest dimension of institutional empire building?

Does anyone, apart from other dinosaurs, discuss 'really useful knowledge', critical intelligence, and consciousness raising? Or reflect upon, with any degree of precision, what it's all about politically? For what purpose are we constructing this Benetton-style solution to educational provision? At what cost in terms of lost community and the disappearance of collective action? And what about feminism? As more and more women are strapped into poverty; our rights attacked, reduced and destroyed by the increasingly arbitrary coercion of the state; with no visible reduction in domestic rates of rape, violence and abuse; are we to assume that the war is over because some women have achieved individual success?

Because it has become usual to mistake imperialism for democracy and the free market for freedom. And because it has become socially and intellectually unsound to speak in essentialist and universal terms about common experiences of oppression, are we still to assume, with a quarter of Europe's poor now living in Britain, and bankruptcies occurring every few minutes, that the best we can do is to adjust the regulations at the margins? I assume that my polemic is not unreasonable. Indeed with the collapse of confidence in Thatcherism, exaggerated by widespread unemployment and disenchantment with the tawdry and gratuitous greed of enterprise economics, the time might well be apposite to reclaim the radical initiative. Maybe others feel the same? I'd be glad to hear from those who do. And to find some ways together of putting the politics of resistance and transformation back onto the agenda of adult and continuing education.

Feminism and women's education

(Originally published in *Adult Learning,*
Critical Intelligence and Social Change,
eds Thompson and Mayo, NIACE 1995)

The deluge of correspondence which greeted Thompson's open letter in Adults
*Learning (see previous chapter) led in 1995 to the publication of **Adult Learning,***
***Critical Intelligence and Social Change** which she co-edited with Marjorie*
*Mayo. As in **Adult Education for a Change** fifteen years earlier, a collection of*
dissident voices from the Left were able to apply critical theories and to outline
alternative priorities to those which currently dominate provision. The book has
helped to inform the agenda of a number of regional meetings and national and
international conferences attended by radical practitioners in adult, continuing and
community education, some of whom, we trust, have the ear of politicians and policy
makers, as well as working in continuing solidarity with students for whom 'really
useful knowledge' and radical learning is still a necessary adjunct to the struggle for
changes in their material and social circumstances, as well as intellectual growth.

In this piece Thompson reviews with the benefit of hindsight the relationship between
continuing education and feminism. Her stance remains that feminism is of little
value as a critical theory if it does not also assist in the process of women's liberation;
and that the purpose of knowledge is not simply to understand the world but also to
change it. She comments on the growth and related demise of academic Women's
Studies in higher education – at a time when more women than ever before are
enrolled in universities – and on the de-radicalising consequences of post-modernism
as an intellectual fashion.

Feminism and women's education

The contribution made by feminism and the Women's Movement to adult and continuing education has been of tremendous importance in the recognition and creation of what counts as 'really useful knowledge'. Not simply in the recent past, in relation to second wave feminism, but also in relation to the educational imperatives of the Suffragettes and Suffragists, the Co-operative Women's Guilds and the early struggles to establish women's trade unions.[1]

In the late 1960s and early 70s the re-emergence of feminism in Britain was encouraged by the general impetus towards critical consciousness and political resistance associated with the spirit of the new Left, Civil Rights and anti imperialism. From its beginnings, in the west at least, in consciousness raising groups and in vociferous political campaigns around equal pay and employment opportunities, contraception and abortion, child care, sexuality, and in opposition to violence against women, the re-emerging Women's Movement was always closely associated with self education and re-education.

It soon became clear to those of us involved, as if blinkers had been taken from our eyes, that prevailing orthodoxy and dominant ideas about women were not natural, or inevitable, or objective. They were socially reproduced. Even the political gurus of the Left, the creators of 'big ideas' like Marx and Lenin and Trotsky, to whom we initially turned for explanations of our social and economic conditions, had developed their theories in circumstances which were seriously flawed by an intrinsic blindness. Received notions of power, oppression, class, freedom of choice and the significance of experience were largely unexamined in terms of gender or ethnicity.

We discovered with astonishment, and then with increasing clarity, that what counted as knowledge, truth and freedom, was built upon a mix of ideology and historical selection, in patriarchal circumstances, based on partial information. Women were 'hidden from history'[2], lost within assumptions that either subsumed women's existence within generalisations about the 'human' condition of 'men' in society, or ignored us completely.[3]

According to Simone de Beauvoir, women existed as 'the other', locked into Enlightenment notions of men's control over culture and women's constraint by nature. Not only different in kind, because of temperament and constitution, but also, in comparison to the 'stronger' sex, deficient, inferior and less significant. With man as norm, women were frequently found wanting, and expected to fulfil a very different kind of destiny.

The Women's Movement rapidly outgrew the un-reconstructed explanations of the Left, and starting from the basis of personal experience, began to re-constitute new understandings and theories about class, gender, 'race', and sexuality. In the process the very nature of politics and knowledge became transformed. Social and personal relations became identified with political activity, in which the domestic and the personal, as well as the structural, became recognised as significant sites of struggle. Sexual politics, as well as socialist politics, became subject to examination and negotiation, in ways that initiated the collapse of simplistic polarities and unqualified economic determinism.

It was not surprising that those of us who were also students and teachers and writers, as well as women with awakening consciousness about our position, carried the impetus and impatience of feminism into our work and into education.

Throughout the 70s and 80s the growing influence and persistence of feminism was an important irritant and source of agitation. Adult Education provided an obvious focus. Although organised and controlled by men, the majority of students were women[4]. The majority of part-time teachers and community education workers, and full-time tutors and organisers in junior positions, were women. The curriculum, although pervasively malestream within the WEA and Extra Mural traditions, relied on received notions of female 'relevance' and 'interest' when it came to Local Authority and community education classes. Nell Keddie[5] pointed to the domesticating and conformist nature of the knowledge offered to women in leisure related and liberal education classes provided by the LEAs. In *Learning Liberation*[6] I drew attention to the concentration on knowledge and assumptions aimed at women which were concerned to adapt us to the logic and requirements of the prevailing system, rather than to assist us in the process of liberation. This recognition, informed by feminism, helped to review the relationship between adult education and 'really useful knowledge'.

The dominant 'liberal tradition' in adult education, associated closely with ideas of 'learning for pleasure' and 'learning for its own sake', was always concerned with 'individual' outcomes and 'personal' growth in the context of predominantly middle class assumptions and value systems. The voices of working class, radical feminism and black consciousness were largely missing from the record.

The 'radical tradition'[7], born out of the concern to overcome the oppressions which locked people into ignorance, poverty and powerlessness, provided an alternative analysis and opportunity. Knowledge that was 'really useful', we believed, would raise awareness; provide ways of analysing and understanding how oppressions were structured and sustained; and would lead to educational and social action for change that was informed by theories derived from collective experience. It became imperative to ensure that this tradition did justice to the political and educational concerns of women and minority groups, as well as those men at 'the cutting edge' of the class struggle.

Feminism demanded the same relationship to knowledge. One which would not simply be about 'personal fulfilment' but about validating women's experience and challenging the imposition of ideas and conditions which worked to oppress women as a group.

Demands for a new kind of 'relevance' was related to the process of 'consciousness raising' and 'changing lives' in a political way, and was also strongly expressed in relation to radical ideas about social class, sexuality, popular activism, adult literacy, black identity and community education.

Out of our criticisms and our re-connections with earlier and more radical roots came a growing dissatisfaction with the prevailing middle class, gendered and liberal culture of the mainstream.

Feminist commitment helped to establish what became quite widespread alternatives. For example, New Opportunities for Women courses, Second Chance, Fresh Start, Women's Studies Programmes, Training in Non Traditional Skills, and Women's Science and New Technology iniatives. The WEA particularly, pioneered a variety of women's political, cultural and trade union courses, as well as assertiveness and self defence courses and women's studies groups. Women's branches were established, a flourishing women's newsletter was produced and a women's organiser was appointed to a senior position at national office that made the Women's Studies programme something of a jewel in the WEA crown by the middle 80s.

Encouraged by the radical wing of the Inner London Education Authority (ILEA) and the Greater London Council (GLC), local authority provision in the capital made equal opportunities a seminal priority. Pioneering work in adult literacy and community education highlighted the need to recognise and respond to class, cultural, ethnic and gender diversity when providing education aimed at the least powerful and most discounted groups within society[8]. Both curriculum development and teaching-learning methods underwent a sustained process of transformation, based on the commitment to student-centred learning, conscientisation[9], and anti-discriminatory practices. In the process feminist ideas and values played an important role. Our own experience in consciousness-raising and study groups, tied to our distrust of patriarchal knowledge, institutionalised authority and leadership, led to the conviction that democratic and collaborative learning relationships were more likely to enhance the self esteem and confidence of women, than traditional, didactic and tutor-dominated methodologies. The influence of feminism usually guaranteed a commitment to equal opportunities and anti-discriminatory practices in general, encouraging levels of awareness and responsiveness which were not nearly so common in mainstream provision.

Some have chosen, in this respect, to pay tribute to the inspiration of Illich[10] and Freire[11], both of whom were sufficiently removed from the more immediate British context and experience to be considered theoretically and practically interesting. But in terms of Women's Studies and women's education, we were already building up our own ideas and ways of working, based on the importance attributed to personal knowledge by the Women's Liberation Movement, the commitment to collectivism, the de-construction of traditional forms of authority and wisdom, and the linking of our developing theories to transforming practice and social change.

In University provision the more enlightened adult education departments all established their 'popular liberation fronts' by the early 80s – some with more conviction than others. At Southampton, for example, the women's education programme grew out of the department's community education programme in the late 70s, in circumstances of initial tolerance but increasing alarm. The contemporary politics and traditional roots which those of us involved used as our inspiration were the notions of women's autonomy and working class independence. In creating the Women's Education Centre in Southampton in 1981, used mostly by working class women, and run on the basis of decision making, participation and control by its members, we weathered an increasingly hostile political decade, during which time the attention of the university became more punitive as we became less dutiful, and as the effects of Thatcherism and New Right thinking became increasingly destructive.

After countless attempts to 'supervise' the politics of the curriculum, 'inspect' the collaborative relationships between the students and the tutors, 'raise' the fees, 'cut' the child care, 'change' the collective organisation to an externally recruited management structure, matters came to a head in 1986. Attempts by the university to withdraw all funding from the creche, sack part-time tutors and require women on benefits to pay course fees, provoked a lively press campaign and vociferous demonstration in support of the Centre's work, which involved former members and sympathetic adult educators nationally, as well as current members of the Centre and their children. The effect of the demonstration and press campaign was to shame the university into making concessions. Of course the authorities blamed the government. But whilst the former freedoms of the universities, the WEA and the LEAs were being systematically reduced, and like other public services, becoming customised and accustomed to the requirements of the market, we continued to sustain our autonomous position for a further five difficult and defiant years[12].

Meanwhile, a more acceptable variety of women's education was gaining ground within the academy, which should not be underestimated. A continuing legacy of second wave feminism has been the development of academic women's studies programmes, which are now established in almost every British university, at both undergraduate and postgraduate levels. It is unlikely that this creation of a new academic specialism would have occurred so quickly and so strongly without the impetus of feminism or the experience provided by developments rooted in adult and community iniatives.

In many ways it has been Access courses which have become the beneficiaries of women's education programmes in the 70s and 80s. No one is any longer in any doubt that considerable numbers of women, presented with the chance of returning to education, will grasp the opportunity with considerable enthusiasm. The rhetoric of Access is still more persuasive than the reality, however, when the costs and consequences of education are measured against the need to earn a living, the regulations surrounding benefits, the dearth and cost of child care support and the total lack of government commitment to providing realistic grants. Yet women have increasingly become the 'targets' in new and expanding education 'markets'. The attempts which many of us made, and the classes which we pioneered in the 80s, in order to make 'really useful knowledge' accessible to 'disadvantaged 'groups, especially working class and black women, have now become an industry. In the process, however, Access has become a fairly middle class affair. No self-respecting FE college is without its Access provision, comprised not exclusively, but predominantly, of lower middle class women. No self-seeking university is without its franchise deals and credit transfer schemes, aimed at maximising its quota of 'non traditional' students within the overall constraints imposed on student numbers. In the process, of course, something of the politics and the passion has been lost. What counts as the culture and the curriculum of Access, what informs the logic of accreditation, what gets assumed in the promotion of APEL[13], for example, owes less to the arguments about cultural politics and critical intelligence, feminism and empowerment, than to the need to generate 'customers' in line with the ideological and political consequences of applying performance indicators and free market economics to the practices of education.

Viewed from the changing political circumstances of the middle 90s, at which point the party political tide is clearly turning, and the present Conservative govern-ment looks much less omnipotent – even to its own supporters – than at any other time in the last fifteen years, it is salutary to consider what we have won and lost, and what we must now do to advance the political and learning interests of women in adult and continuing education.

1979 was the year in which Gloria Gaynor provided the still quite youthful, born again and politically unsophisticated Women's Movement with one of its contemporary anthems – 'I Will Survive'. It was also the year which saw the inaugura-tion of Margaret Thatcher as Britain's first woman Prime Minister. Those who had their wits about them could see that this was no ordinary chop and change of govern-ment. I can remember being at a meeting about funding for a women's education project, in a room rented from the Labour Party, at which a woman stood up and spoke passionately and eloquently about the severity of the impending backlash. We listened, mesmerised by the conviction and implications of her warnings. But we thought that she exaggerated. Like almost every other 'innocent abroad' we were unprepared for the degree, the disdain, the daring and the destruction which was to accompany the relentless resurgence of the 'radical' Right.

As the 80s progressed, the women who signed up for a Second Chance in education, a Fresh Start, or a New Opportunity, got both 'richer' and poorer. Women from those cultural and social groups which were already well represented in adult education provision began to take advantage of Access and women-centred courses which were much more relevant and responsive to the concerns of women seeking education as distinct from transitory diversions and trivial pursuits. When fees were required, they paid them.

At the Women's Education Centre in Southampton we continued to give prior-ity to working class and unwaged women and to keep the costs of coming to an absolute minimum. Those who joined our classes did so with greater difficulty, in spite of mounting obstacles, in relation to growing desperation and with dwindling expectations, as the decade wore on. The numbers of women living in poverty, on their own with children, under the scrutiny of the state, and in a climate of reaction to the ideas and concerns of feminism increased in direct relation to monetarist economic policies, cuts in benefits and public services, the buoyancy of right wing ideology and increasing levels of unemployment.

As the political issues for working class, unwaged and black women became increasingly determined by the feminisation and racialisation of poverty, the restructuring of the economy, and the restructuring of the welfare state, the response of adult education displayed a growing tension between its own struggle to survive government cuts and reorganisation, and feminist attempts to hang onto scarce resources for women's education.

Faced with education institutions reneging on their previous commitments to community education and to the poor, equal opportunities iniatives became as out of date as popular democracy in quangoland. In this respect, some feminists, like many erstwhile social and cultural workers, became advocates and exponents of the 'new realism' and took the line of least resistance.

One of the problems with the liberal and middle class domination of the early Women's Movement, as many black and lesbian and working class women had already begun to point out, was the confusion in loyalties caused by professional status and some residual allegiance to the rules and regulations of the men in mainstream organisations. Such was the hostility displayed towards 'extremism' , the ridicule attached to left wing 'lunacy', and the irrelevance attributed to feminism – provoked by the New Right, cultivated by the media, and largely undefended by the Liberal Left – that many wavered and collapsed against the strain.

But it would be unfair of me to blame feminism for failing to defend women's education from the material and ideological assault of 'radical' Right thinking and policy requirements – policies which also made virtual mincemeat of local government democracy, trade union rights, the health and welfare services and the pursuit of critical intelligence as distinct from training. Feminism, it was said, was no longer necessary, now that the only deterrent to women's equal opportunities was our own inertia. Tokenism in high places, supported by competitive individualism and libertarian propaganda welcomed in the 'post-feminist' age. Part of the logic of New Right strategies was to co-opt, neutralise and discredit potential sources of opposition, like feminism, and to wipe from the collective consciousness the memory of subversive movements which might give a voice to resistance and provide real evidence of alternative ideas and ways of operating.

Within universities the preoccupations of many academics became distracted by the passing intellectual fashion called post-modernism, which in turn became entrenched in some Women's Studies courses.[14] The re-classification of Women's Studies into Gender Studies began, and the debates became increasingly obscure, fragmented and particular. Courses were increasingly put together by those who had no roots in the resurgence of feminism, no experience of front line feminist politics, no interest, as far as one could tell, in praxis. The intellectual sophistication of feminist derived theories soon placed them above reproach in the male academy, however, measured by the proliferation of publications, the erudition of their scholarship, and the growing numbers of students choosing to study them. It was not long before men also joined the queue to teach about women and gender in relation, for example, to masculinity, identity and sexuality. It looked as though 'feminist knowledge' had at last arrived.

Increasingly, however, the arguments of post-modernism were used to make intellectual sense of the alleged fragmentation of the western women's movement, just at the moment when issues to do with class, ethnicity, social difference and sexuality were being most fiercely contested. Except that the obscurity of the endeavour frequently appeared more alienating and immaterial to women's lives than the ill-formulated but well intentioned essentialism it sought to displace.

The arrival of Women's Studies and Gender Studies in universities and colleges has been, of course, an achievement to be relished. It is no longer so possible for patriarchal institutions to retain their distinct privileges and powerful influence over the intellectual reproduction of malestream ideas once women have begun to occupy positions of leadership and initiative. But the battles are far from over.

Whilst Audre Lorde[15] was warning of the dangers of incorporation (in the original, political sense of the term), insisting that 'the master's tools will never dismantle the master's house', others of a radical persuasion also disputed the effectiveness of strategies based on becoming 'dutiful daughters'[16] and seeking recognition by demonstrations of relentless reasonableness and moderation in the face of continuing sexism, or by lending credibility to tokenism.[17]

The promotion of selected women in systems sustained by men revealed that recognition often had its price. The price was gratitude, loyalty and obligation. Too often they provided the examples set to others, the role models, the evidence of opportunity that closed the doors on more serious or fundamental challenge. Too often those who 'made it' lent credibility to an otherwise continuing concentration of white male control. But in 1994, ten years after 'power dressing' had become an art form practised by new style femocrats, and 'Women into Management' courses had become an outpost of the enterprise culture, the numbers of women in key management positions in industry had again begun to fall, and the numbers of women who had broken through the academic glass ceiling, in ways that have helped to transform the patriarchal nature, culture and control of education, remained few and far between.

And none of which has done very much to advance the interests of the majority of women in society, whose material circumstances and access to equal opportunities actually deteriorated as the Thatcher years ground on.

In these circumstances, the attachment to post-modernist approaches among some academic feminists has done little to assist in the struggles that have preoccupied the vast majority of women. A well known convert to the new orthodoxy has been Michele Barrett, former Marxist feminist, now writing books with Anne Philips like *Destabilizing Theory: Contemporary Feminist Debates*, which turns out not to be about a range of feminisms, as one might expect, but which is exclusively about post modernism. According to Stevi Jackson[18] 'the points of reference for most post modernist feminists are not other feminists, but theorists such as Lacan, Derrida and Foucault'. It is not simply that 'these are men', and therefore 'to be avoided' but that they are men who speak from a position which is not sympathetic to feminism. Their influence may have helped to provide some temporary kudos to women disciples in the male-dominated academy, but their influence has played into the hands of those who are pleased to see Women's Studies de-radicalised, who find the study of gender less challenging, and who have no particular interest in women's liberation. The concerns of post modernism – to do with linguistics, culture and identity – are far from accessible to the general feminist reader. And in their most extreme expression come with a denial of any form of material reality.

The function of the feminist curriculum in education should not have been to obscure, to mystify and to restrict entry into its insights. Otherwise it becomes a self-indulgent, inward looking, élite activity, that acts to exclude others, rather than enable them to learn. The feminist curriculum, as it relates to the concerns of women in the workplace, in low paid employment and the home, must be grounded in the experiences, the victories, the problems, and the aspirations of women surviving in these situations. All of which are immensely serious material realities. Grounded in such a way as to make connections with the lives of other women, to make political sense of everyday experience, to develop understandings that enhance consciousness and which lead to political and social action for change. Given the discrepancies of wealth and power between North and South, the growth of fundamentalism, the re-emergence of nationalism and the fairly basic inequalities between men and women revealed daily in the re-constitution of Eastern Central Europe – it is imperative to do this in a context which transcends ethnocentric and particularist dimensions. Not in the post modern sense of neo-pluralism but in recognition of complexity and difference as well as commonality.

In these circumstances women's education is most useful when it is concerned not with post-modernism but with 'really useful knowledge'. The kind of knowledge that supports women, in the company of others, in the business of transforming our lives. The kind of knowledge that shifts the emphasis from victims to survivors. From customers to activists. From impotence to creative anger. From those who desist to those who resist. The kind of knowledge that assists women in various and real sites of struggle, including those which are personal and private, to confront the everyday experiences of inequality and power relations which help sustain the logic and the authority of the status quo. In other words, to help women bring about change, in historical circumstances which may not be conducive, but in ways that are a matter of survival.

In declaring the death of 'big ideas' and of historical and structural explanations of social inequality and power, post modernism has, in my view gone too far. Certainly it was appropriate to recognise the politics of difference and diversity, and to underline the many ways in which global theories of social progress and social change are flawed by simplification, inconsistencies and contradictions. These are, after all, the same theories that second wave feminists had already begun to challenge in terms of their silences and misrepresentations about women.

But in providing the philosophy to explain the end of totalitarian categories, in favour of more local narratives and multifarious identities, and helping to legitimise emerging ideologies associated with free choice, free market economics and free enterprise, writers like Lyotard[19] and Vattimo[20] in seeking to challenge much of what was previously 'taken for granted' have, in the process, acted as a mirror image of the wider political and economic movement to the Right.

The intellectual enthusiasm for post-modernism among some academic feminists needs to be properly understood. At worst it has become a revitalised agenda in favour of relativism and pluralism. A collapse into individualistic reductionism that could destroy the possibility of collective action and suppresses political will. In which the concept of power, influenced by the ideas of Foucault, has been displaced into the spaces between minimal encounters, and the disparate exchanges and negotiations of everyday life. At best it simply confirms what feminists have always said about the personal nature of the political, in which large issues both grow out of and get reproduced in small ways, in the day-to-day negotiation of relationships based on unequal amounts of power. But to invert the telescope, as post-modernism then chooses to do, to consider the particular in the foreground, without registering the collective, material, deep seated impact of the structures in the background, is to ignore the strength and influences of forces that help to shape the conditions in which the particular happens. The refusal to consider 'big' questions on the grounds that 'global categories are inaccurate', and 'there is no such thing as certainty or truth' is, of course, politically convenient for those who benefit from power on a big scale. If discrepancies based on 'race', wealth, power and gender can no longer be addressed, how can there be any effective challenge to social, sexual and economic systems that distribute their rewards and penalties unequally? It is clearly premature to speak about the death of grand narratives in relation to the significance of capitalism and patriarchy, for example, when both sources of power so obviously continue to be reproduced and re-constituted.

When earlier feminists talked of patriarchy, it might have seemed like the kind of ahistorical, culturally specific, grandiose kind of concept that distorted the significance of other oppressions, such as racism and imperialism, in ways that made resistance or change seem impossible. But these were grounds for refining and developing our theories, and using words more carefully. Not for defining out and distracting attention away from the nature and predominance of male power.

Put plainly, the issue is a question of political significance. Does the shift from structural, economic, patriarchal and political explanations of women's subordination, towards subjective, cultural and linguistic preoccupations with the character, style, and meaning of identity, for example, advance or paralyse the possibility of women's independence? I suspect the former seems too big to contemplate, the latter seems too small to matter. In practice we cannot afford to abandon either. Systems of oppression, like experience, require both de-construction and re-construction in the interests of our liberation.

The amelioration and transformation of women's material circumstances requires political consciousness, political resistance and political action. It also requires courage. The somewhat philosophical and linguistic preoccupation of post-modernism has helped to divert some varieties of academic feminism away from being a subversive social movement, aligned to the Women's Liberation Movement, and engaged in direct action; in favour of a cerebral, inward looking, élite activity, that denies the possibility of widespread transformation brought about by committed social and political action for change. In such circumstances it is vital to hold onto the lessons that earlier feminist ideas have taught us, in order to continue to relate political consciousness and understanding to the lived experiences of the vast majority of women. Women who, in different cultures and different circumstances, still have to make sense of the world from positions of low pay, no pay, racism and poverty. Women whose capacity for survival, and whose potential for resistance, is not in question but who can be assisted by the ideas and information that rescue women's lives from oblivion, that make connections between women, in ways that 'name the enemy' and 'shift the blame' from themselves and each other, onto forces much more powerful than the pathology of individuals.

Teaching Women's Studies at Ruskin, as I now do, underlines all the problems associated with building and sustaining a vision of alternative practice in the current educational and political climate.

Ostensibly Ruskin has much to recommend it. It has a history closely associated, in the literature of adult education at least, with the radical tradition, reflecting across the years the tension between education as a tool of liberation and an instrument of social control. But its commitment to working class constituencies, to socialism and the labour movement, and in turn to women, has always been contradictory. In 1909 the Plebs Strike drew attention to Ruskin's ambiguous position in relation to 'really useful knowledge' and to Oxford University. The Plebs League was a socialist fraternity, which although inspired by Marxist politics, was itself quite authoritarian[21] and sexist. In February 1970 the first National Women's Liberation Conference chose Ruskin as its venue but feminism didn't enter the College curriculum until over twenty years later. In 1976 the College provided the speaking opportunity for James Callaghan, the then Labour Prime Minister, to lay the groundwork for subsequent Conservative education policies, concerned to narrow the curriculum, and direct the attention of education towards the needs of industry.

Like the best and worst of those in the organised labour movement, it has taken Ruskin as long as any on the Left, to come to terms with the contradictions of the old left and those who are the 'post-modernisers' and to acknowledge the different concerns of women and black people in narrow definitions of the class struggle.

In such circumstances, the prospect of students learning about feminism, a curriculum which recognises both structural oppression and cultural diversity, which prioritises women's experiences of the world, and insists upon confronting prejudice and developing anti-discriminatory practices, all provide real challenges to closed minds and vested academic interests – even in a College like Ruskin. It also challenges the workerist mentality and crude patriarchal priorities of some of its more traditional students. Issues to do with unreconstructed masculinity and sexual harassment are probably no more endemic at Ruskin than other organisations in which men and women work together, but the increasing presence of Women's Studies students and the declared intention to 'shift the culture' of the College as well as the curriculum, means that life in a residential community is far from being a simply academic affair.

At the same time, the ongoing pressure from the government, fronted by the Further Education Funding Council, remains determined to draw the residential adult colleges into the same market-driven, cost-cutting, commercialised system of provision, in which others in adult and continuing education have already been forced to operate. It is not a system which encourages critical thinking or cultural resistance. Quite the reverse.

Dogged by the Old Left and bullied by the New Right, it is still not an easy time to be speaking of feminist knowledge, or holding onto learning principles about asking questions as distinct from collecting credits. At a recent conference organised by NIACE on Quality Assurance in Education[22], Terry Melia of the FEFC boasted about his ability to 'grade everything that moves on a five point scale'. And as Cilla Ross[23] argues, part of the consequence of modularisation, accreditation and quality control has been the simplification and the acceleration of the time set aside for critical thinking. With adult students who have missed out on previous educational success, this represents yet another deprivation. GNVQs in Further Education have already made a mission out of multiple choice answers, that can be reduced to ticks on sheets, which can then be marked by a machine. In adult and continuing education, increasing variations on meaningless qualifications proliferate, like so much confetti, whilst no one has required Oxbridge to modularise, accelerate or standardise its courses.

In this kind of climate, it is just as important as it ever was in women's education to make the subject matter of what is learned, relate to the cultural, material and political condition of women's lives. And to the expectation of our liberation.[24] Otherwise we collude in reducing women's experiences to silence or absence in the guise of brevity. We collude in keeping women in their place, attuned to the logic of an unequal and oppressive society.

In the development of the Women's Studies programme at Ruskin we are using the history and intensity of the recent past, and what has happened to women as the starting point from which to rebuild the road to feminism. It means repeating and relearning many of the lessons we thought we'd learned already. It means making sure that women, many of whom don't remember much about life before Thatcher, know that they come from other, deeper roots, with traditions that are based on resilience and courage; and from generations of women who have experienced victories and triumphs as well as defeats. It means learning not simply academic knowledge, devoid of political significance and purpose, but seeing knowledge as a tool which can be used to raise awareness and provoke resistance. It means un-learning the rules of competitive individualism prescribed by the proponents of the New Right in favour of collective learning and collaboration. It means not always looking for a leader but becoming oneself an activist, who knows that it takes trouble and it takes courage to be free. It means, as it always did, seeking the connections between the things we know from within ourselves; how these relate to the experiences of others; building theories to understand the world more clearly as a consequence; and finding the courage to make the difference.

In this way the feminist curriculum, when it is focused with precision, understanding and illumination, can assist in the process of consciousness raising and social transformation; which remains, and continues to be, the first lines of defence against the persistence of inequality and oppression.

Notes and References

1. Jane Thompson, *Learning Liberation: Women's Response to Men's Education*, (Croom Helm, 1983).
2. Sheila Rowbotham, *Hidden From History*, (Pluto, 1973).
3. Dale Spender, *Women of Ideas*, (RKP 1982).
4. Thompson 1983 op cit
5. Nell Keddie, Adult Education: An Ideology of Individualism, in Thompson (ed.) *Adult Education For A Change*, (Hutchinson, 1980).
6. Thompson 1983 op cit
7. Richard Johnson, Really Useful Knowledge: Radical Education and Working Class Culture in Clarke, Critcher and Johnson (eds) *Working Class Culture: Studies in History and Theory*, (Hutchinson, 1979).
8. Rebecca O'Rourke, All Equal Now?, in (ed) Thompson and Mayo, *Adult Learning, Critical Intelligence and Social Change*, (NIACE 1995).
9. Paulo Freire, *Pedagogy of the Oppressed*, (Harmondsworth: Penguin, 1972).
10. Ivan Illich, *Deschooling Society*, (Harmondsworth : Penguin, 1973)
11. Freire op cit
12. Taking Liberties Collective, *Learning the Hard Way: Women's Oppression in Men's Education*, (MacMillan, 1989)
13. Wilma Fraser, *Making Experience Count – Towards What?*, in (ed) Thompson and Mayo 1995
14. Stevi Jackson, The Amazing Deconstructing Woman, in *Trouble and Strife* (25,1992).
15. Audre Lorde, The Master's Tools will Never Dismantle the Master's House, in (ed) Moraga, Anzaldua, *This Bridge Called My Back*, (Persephone Press, 1981).
16. Adrienne Rich, Towards a Woman Centred University, in *On Lies Secrets and Silences, Selected Prose 1966–78*, (Virago 1980).
17. Taking Liberties Collective, op cit.
18. Jackson op cit
19. J.F. Lyotard, *The Post Modern Condition: A Report on Knowledge*, (Minnesota University Press, 1984)
20. G. Vatimo, *The End of Modernity: Nihilism and Hermeneutics in Post Modern Culture*, (Polity Press, 1988)
21. Geoff Brown, Independence and Incorporation: The Labour College Movement and the WEA before the Second World War, in Thompson (ed) *Adult Education for a Change*, 1980.
22. Quality Matters, NIACE conference, London, November 1993
23. Cilla Ross, *Seizing the Quality Initiative: Regeneration and the Radical Project*, in (ed) Thompson and Mayo 1995.
24. Thompson 1983 op cit

The great tradition:
a personal reflection

(Originally Published in *Liberal Adult Education:
The End of an Era*, ed John Wallis,
Continuing Education Press, Nottingham University 1996)

*In 1996 Nottingham University published **Liberal Adult Education: The End of
an Era** in order to pay tribute to the passing of the liberal tradition in adult education
and the contribution which some of its eminent professors had made to it. Thompson
had never been a fan of the tradition or of the ways in which she thought it helped to
individualise and de-radicalise adult learning in relation to social change. However,
the residual liberalism of the institution prevailed, and her observations were reflected
in the valedictory. In this piece her contribution implies little sympathy for the passing
of the tradition, or its wider influence on the liberal culture of adult education pre-
Thatcher, because, as she argues, it helped to prepare the ground for the wholesale
shift towards rampant individualism, consumerism and market thinking that
determined the educational policies of the New Right. It was allowed to flounder by
generations of students who in their pre-occupation with 'learning for personal
pleasure' or engaging with the kinds of scholarship which was alleged to be 'the best
that has been thought and said', they had not developed any strong allegiance to an
adult education movement which they would seek collectively to defend. This essay
was also presented as background reading in relation to her contribution to the
conference on Emancipatory Learning and Social Change in Sydney in September
1995.*

The great tradition:
a personal reflection

In a world in which many adult education workers either 'mourn the passing' or 'do not remember' much about the heady days (*sic*) of adult education before the Thatcher-Major onslaught – it seems important, in the context of a collection like this, to remind ourselves about some of the limitations of the so called 'Great Tradition', in case a kind of ritual eulogy to the words and wisdom of Harold Wiltshire *et al* serves to obscure or romanticise a far from perfect past.

My reflections are not those of an academic theorist, concerned about the nature and meaning of liberal adult education in its philosophical context, so much as the experience and analysis of one whose purpose and practice as an adult educator has been developed and clarified in the context of profound irritation with the liberal tradition and growing opposition to the new vocationalism which has largely replaced it.

Having lived through a period of considerable economic and social restructuring – I am writing in October 1994 – and of changes which have not simply affected education but are epitomised in what is often referred to as a 'paradigm shift' in both the thinking and practice of education, there is again a feeling of change in the air. Not particularly because there is much to be optimistic about in the educational policy statements emanating from New Labour or the recommendations of the Commission for Social Justice but more because the almost 'absolute' and 'divine right to rule' assumed by successive Tory governments in recent years, and translated into a near totalitarian political orthodoxy in the eighties by the relentlessness of Thatcherism, has at last begin to crumble. Despite the ongoing efforts of the Tory Right to place a further stretch of 'clear blue water' between themselves and any likely competition for the middle ground in British politics, the momentum which a few years ago seemed to be unstoppable, is now in a state of collapse. Even in its own terms – to do with traditional values, rewarding individual initiative, self styled occupation of the high moral ground and business enterprise, the Thatcher legacy is becoming tainted and less effective than it once was. There is space around the edges once again, and even in the more traditional heartlands, for mobilising effective opposition.[1]

As politicians begin to re-group, and new arrangements are invented to make sense of national and international responses to post communism, late capitalism and globalisation – the cultural and ideological role of education as a crucial and contested site of struggle needs to be understood, debated and practised with the conviction that, what each of us is able to do, either contributes to or detracts from our visions of what might happen next, at this important moment of historical change. The recognition of the relationship between education and activism expressed by Paulo Freire in *Pedagogy of the Oppressed*[2] is still as relevant today,

> *Education either functions as an instrument which is used to facilitate the integration of generations into the logic of the present system and bring about conformity to it, or it becomes 'the practice of freedom', the means by which men and women deal critically and creatively with reality and discover how to participate in the transformation of their world.*

The liberal tradition in adult education, sometimes referred to as the Great Tradition, also had its philosophy and visions, as others in this collection will explain. Measured against the rather pragmatic, materialistic, and cost-effective criteria of market derived and market-driven preoccupations of recent years, it has become commonplace in the fringe meetings of local gatherings and national conferences, to hear beleaguered and nostalgic expressions of regret from those old enough to remember a time before Thatcher, when the language of 'learning for its own sake', 'learning for pleasure' and 'responding to students' needs' was part of the everyday understanding of liberal adult education workers.

Bombarded more recently on all sides by funding related accreditation schemes, marketing strategies, performance indicators, quality control requirements and competency criteria – a new language has been developed which has made it increasingly more difficult to talk about students and adult learners as distinct from customers and unit costs; to talk about the meaning and purpose of education as distinct from strategic plans and mission statements; to talk about the nature of the curriculum and appropriate teaching methods as distinct from modularisation and appraisal mechanisms; to talk about equal opportunities as distinct from student numbers; to talk about thinking and questioning as distinct from measuring and monitoring. As the very concept of 'adult education' disappears from official descriptions of educational policy, the practice of adult education also becomes increasingly difficult to distinguish and sustain. Keith Jackson[3] reminds us about the senior civil servant's telling paraphrase of Thatcher's own apocryphal vision of society, 'there is no such thing as adult education today, only adults attending classes'.

In this kind of context, nostalgia for a time when the so called 'pleasure' and 'confidence' alleged to derive from flower arranging and cake decorating classes, often led to a life transformed by adult education, in which the progression to more challenging academic experiences was held to be commonplace. It was a time when 'the best that has been thought and said' and which was thought to be enshrined in university-based knowledge, was extended beyond the boundaries of the academy to those 'in the community' through extra mural and voluntary body provision, so they could also experience 'high status' knowledge, with its alleged capacity to cultivate individual enlightenment, civilisation, and personal fulfilment in 'the true spirit' of a democratic society. Justifications and idealisations which now have an immensely 'faded former era' feel about them, but which linger in apparent contrast to the current preoccupations with credit accumulation and transfer schemes, operating like banks in an inflationary economy, to print currency like confetti, and create qualifications that are hardly worth the paper they're printed on, except as a major diversion from a different kind of analysis about what is really going on.

My purpose here is not to de-construct the new educational language and institutional changes, which so many former liberals, and indeed socialists, in adult education have seemingly been eager to adopt, as an indication of their recognition of 'realism' during the Thatcher and Major years, except to note that it has happened.[4] But to suggest that this shift in paradigm, this systematic accommodation to the language and policies of the New Right has found those in adult education to be much more amenable, on the whole, to its logic and demands than school teachers have been prepared to be.

If the shifts in emphasis which have been brought about in adult and continuing education are viewed in the general context of New Right attempts to remake all manner of public services, including the health service and social services, into business enterprises, governed by the so-called logic of the market; and to undermine potential sources of considered opposition like local authorities and trade unions; and to reduce the opportunities for democratic accountability in favour of various unaccountable quangos, leaving little to choose between the organisation and ethos of privatised and regulatory bodies like Oftel (in relation to British Telecom) and Ofsted (in relation to education); then the energetic and enthusiastic acceptance of government directives by adult educators concerned to engage *more* students in *less* face-to-face teaching and critical thinking, in the name of modularisation, 'flexible learning', 'self directed study' and dubious academic and vocational qualifications, is hardly the radical collective response to these measures we might have hoped for.

The extent and enthusiasm of the response by adult education workers to what amounts to a serious attack on the potentially radical and critical role of adult education both to inform and assist in the process of democratic participation, social liberation, and political transformation, is in my view a direct consequence of the previous enthusiasm of adult education workers for the liberal tradition. In other words, the Great Tradition as it developed, and as it was provided in the heady days before Thatcher, helped to *lay the foundations* and *prepare the way* for what was then to be an unseemly rush to the Right, which through a series of decisive cuts and government policy directives, soon proceeded to relegate its insignificance to history.

My first experience of adult education happened in Hull, in a working class comprehensive school, in the early 1970s. The school was a concrete and glass monstrosity, a short bus ride from where I grew up before going to university. It was built on the remains of a bomb site, in the only square space of unoccupied land between factories and terrace houses, packed cheek by jowl between the docks and a maximin security prison. But it was 1970. The women's liberation group I joined (whatever happened to liberation?) joined with Lily Bilocca to relate the emergence of second wave feminism to the class struggle, and in particular the campaign led by fishermen's wives to get radio systems installed on trawlers in a year when ships and men were lost without trace in the perilous fishing grounds off Iceland. As a group we clubbed together to send one of our members to the first National Women's Liberation conference at Ruskin College in February and knew, when she returned, that we were in some sense 'making history'.

During the day I introduced working class kids destined for the trawlers, Reckitt and Colmans and the Metal Box factory to the study of sociology, just as O and A levels in the subject were being invented and whilst sociology was still considerably identified with the New Left and student politics of the late 60s.

These were 'the days of miracles and wonder' when IMG, Civil Rights, Anti-Vietnam War demonstrations and the re-emergence of feminism were formative influences on a generation of first generation recruits into 'lesser professional' jobs as cultural workers. When left wing intellectuals joined with the members of the working class in community education and development projects to try to make the state more accountable to the concerns of working class people in the belief that information, agitation and collaboration in a democratic society was what led to social change.

At night in the comprehensive school I worked with the tutor organiser for the WEA to provide a range of evening meetings, political workshops, short courses and conferences for local people, on issues to do with housing rights, education, community action campaigns and economic issues. Together we produced a newspaper; we ran a conference about equal opportunities in education in the days when the abolition of streaming and mixed ability teaching were signs of progress; and got parents involved in public planning meetings, oral history projects and worker-writer groups. He was said to be a communist by his colleagues. I had no idea that what we were doing was progressive in conventional adult education circles.

By the time I was appointed to the adult education department at Southampton University, as Lecturer in Community Education, I had considerable understanding, from my own background and my previous work, about the relationship between social class, the mal-distribution of power and resources in society, and the role of adult education as a necessary provider of the kind of learning identified by Richard Johnson in earlier times as 'really useful knowledge'[5] In the nineteenth century, in the pages of the Poor Man's Guardian, this meant knowledge that sought to make sense of the causes of hardship and oppression in working class people's lives,

> . . . to enable men to judge correctly of the real causes of misery and distress
> so prevalent . . . to consider what remedies will prove most effectual in
> removing the causes of those evils so that the moral and political influence of
> the people may be united for the purpose of supporting such measures as are
> really calculated to improve their condition.[6]

As myself and others have argued frequently elsewhere, and most recently in *Adult Education, Critical Intelligence and Social Change*[7], this concept remains crucial in contemporary circumstances because it implies knowledge which connects the cultural with the intellectual and the practical, makes no crude distinctions between what is vocational and non-vocational, and depends for its curriculum on the material concerns and political interests of those for whom education cannot be seen as the luxury of leisure or progression, but must help to make sense of intolerable circumstances with a view to changing them.

Three years prior to my appointment at Southampton, the Russell Report had argued that there was a strong case for expanding adult education provision to 'the socially and culturally deprived, living in urban areas' which would often have an 'experimental and informal character'. The Russell Report was part of the same momentum which produced a decade of reports into eg town planning (Skeffington), primary education (Plowden), the personal social services (Seebohm) etc, and which were responding to perceived failures in the structures and processes of the welfare state. Russell shared with these other reports the basic assumption that the political economy of the welfare state was not itself problematic. As Jackson points out[8]

> there was no break with the consensus which had dominated public policy since the 1940s, namely that the fundamental problems of a capitalist political economy had been resolved by a balance of class forces, with the state acting as a means of regulating the economy in order to ensure full employment and social justice. In seeking to tidy up the edges of the welfare state none of the reports considered that the problems they were addressing might be manifestations of a more fundamental crisis in the political economy.

Russell in its turn recommended a variety of 'experimental' and interventionist gestures which gave rise to a spate of community adult education projects in the decade which followed. Such was the Southampton department's New Communities Project[9] in the hinterland of Portsmouth and which initiative I was appointed to develop.

In practice I was unprepared for how pervasively the liberal assumptions of the Great Tradition – inherent in the working practices of the department, in which key individuals had learned their trade in Nottingham at the feet of Harold Wiltshire – had shaped the formulation and assessment of what the research revealed. Nowhere in the published findings of the research, or in the plans for the future, was there any significant analysis of class or gender, or any recognition that what could be counted on as education in the project was being used as a diversion, a form of 'second rate' knowledge, concerned as one resident put it to 'keep the buggers happy', and justified in terms of being 'less threatening'. It was clearly just another form of social control rather than a means of personal and collective liberation which paid serious attention to the serious circumstances in which many in the community were forced to live. Theoretical references to the works of Illich and Freire remained theoretical and locked into the safety of foreign contexts which were sufficiently removed from the day to day reality of downtown Southampton and Portsmouth in the middle seventies to be found interesting but not applicable.

I think my appointment was generally viewed by those who made it as something of a mistake judging by the amount of resistance I subsequently encountered to the deployment of a Marxist, and increasingly, a feminist analysis. In the wake of publications I was associated with like *Adult Education For a Change*[10] and *Learning Liberation*[11] the full weight of the Department's liberal tradition rallied behind notions of 'educational neutrality', 'academic objectivity', the 'tutorial tradition' and a highly particular (ie dead, white, male, middle class and European) selection of knowledge and culture confirmed as 'truth'.

I recount this now not to pick away at old scars or to settle old scores but as an illustration of one of the most significant limitations of the liberal tradition – its profound resistance to any form of structural or material explanations of social and educational inequality or educational élitism. Because it was alleged that 'access to adult education' was 'open to all', and because it was assumed that any failure on the part of potential students to participate was either to do with their cultural deficiency[12] or inefficient advertising and recruitment procedures on the part of institutions[13], the cultural control of adult education by dominant forms of knowledge and ideology, and its appropriation by those with already huge amounts of middle class cultural capital, was taken for granted.

There were of course voices of dissent – many of those who contributed to *Adult Education for a Change*, for example, and who worked in grim urban neighbourhoods, trade union meeting places and community projects – trying to relate the acquisition of 'really useful knowledge' and critical intelligence to intellectual understanding and collective social action. Working in the kind of contexts and with the kind of students which those enmeshed in the Great Tradition rarely encountered, except as occasional and idiosyncratic individuals who defied all sociological generalisations and occasionally found their way into tutorial classes as token workers.

The liberal tradition, of course, did not recognise as a problem the middle class bias of the student body, or the implicitly élitist assumptions built into the selection and delivery of the curriculum. Nor did it recognise until it was pointed out by commentators like Nell Keddie and myself how individualistic and selective were its perspectives. The fact that large numbers of organisers and tutors at university level were men and large numbers of students were women went largely unnoticed until Keddie pointed to the ways in which the organisation and curriculum of liberal adult education operated according to an ideology of individualism which acted to conform women students particularly to the logic of the status quo.[14] In *Learning Liberation* I commented on the extent to which the liberal tradition reflected the selection of knowledge and teaching methods established historically by white middle class men and which in the process ignored or silenced the material, gender and cultural concerns of working class people, women and ethnic minority groups. Despite sweeping claims laid to universal qualities of reason, truth, enlightenment and democracy, the voices of the powerless, including working class and black people, the unemployed, lesbians and gay men and women speaking in their own right were largely missing from the classrooms of the Great Tradition.

Throughout the 1970s and 1980s it was not tutorial classes in 'Chaucer and his Times' or 'Medieval Castles' which registered the significance of adult education as an activity worth defending when the cuts began. Although defined as 'marginal' it was the work done by people like Keith Jackson and Martin Yarnit in Liverpool[15] and Tom Lovett in Northern Ireland[16] which sought to re-constitute the resources of the Great Tradition, as symbolic of a particular kind of intellectual property which needed to be socialised and radicalised and redistributed in more appropriate and democratic forms to those who were excluded from its privileges – using very similar kinds of arguments to those which influenced the establishment of Ruskin College and the Labour College Movement.[17] The same arguments which characterised the 19th century radical tradition, seeking the kind of knowledge that would help to 'get us out of our present troubles'.[18] The kind of knowledge that was related to the material, social, political and cultural conditions of working class life, which could provide insight and understanding, which could provide a critical analysis of systems of oppression privilege and power and which might assist people in their collective efforts to make changes. It was this kind of knowledge and purpose which fitted very well with trade union education, with feminist education, with community action, with equal opportunities initiatives and with anti racist strategies in the 70s and 80s[19] – all of which offered contemporary reincarnations of traditional radical concerns to treat education as a tool of liberation rather than a means of élitist reproduction and social control.

When the New Right arrived the Great Tradition was ill-prepared to make any other response except capitulation. Living comfortably on the periphery of university life for many years, extra mural departments enjoyed all the privileges of academic life and avoided most of the internal rivalries. Whilst some academics from intra mural departments looked down on extra mural departments as being 'not quite scholarly enough', and some extra mural academics looked down on WEA tutors as being 'not quite scholarly enough', and all of them looked down on LEA provision as dealing in hobbies and remedial education, the New Right arrived to produce the inevitable shake up. When research profiles and funding, profit and cost efficiency became the order of the day, adult education departments became vulnerable. The long standing complacency and élitism of the Great Tradition was in itself found wanting by comparison to the more aggressive machismo of intra mural centres of alleged excellence. Once deficit funding was replaced by financial targets, the last vestiges of pretence about 'learning for its own sake' and knowledge that constituted 'the best which had been thought and said' were jettisoned in the search for new markets – any markets – and for commodities that could be packaged and sold in ways that would provide income.[20]

Continuing education sought to distance itself from adult education and the liberal tradition and took on a very different meaning and remit from that of 'lifelong learning'. In universities up and down the land continuing education became synonymous with award bearing qualifications and with those professions and individuals who could pay to have themselves 'up graded', 'refreshed' and 'requalified'. Management training, frequently related to specific vocational areas, became a minor empire. That and franchise deals with lower status institutions to promote Access Courses which would help to supply increasing numbers of 'non-traditional students' to comply with government directives and the necessary 'bums on seats' to meet funding requirements. In the process, worthy but financially unviable provision was scrapped, as was labour-intensive, non profit-making, troublesome and contentious work, promoted by those whose institutional loyalty (as distinct from loyalty to working class and disempowered communities) and conversion to 'new realism' could not be guaranteed

In 1986, three weeks into a new term of a year-long 'Second Chance' programme for working class women, most of whom were single parents and living on benefits in down town Southampton, the University Department responsible for its funding decided, without any consultation, to close down the crèche, sack part-time tutors and insist that all course fees be found in full. It took a well attended demonstration and a national press campaign to shame the department into restoring its financial commitment to the course[21] but not without the organising tutor, who was alleged to have brainwashed around 200 women and children into demonstrating on behalf of women's education, from being disciplined for 'professional disloyalty' to the university.[22]

Of course the Great Tradition, like many other relics of former, more consensual times, like trade union politics and local council democracy, was 'on the run' from the New Right. But as a measure of its support in academia and in the wider community, very little in the way of demonstrations and national press campaigns were mounted in its support. Whatever 'learning' it had helped to provide 'for pleasure' or 'for its own sake' across the years, it had not been sufficient to turn an essentially individualistic uncommitted student body into a vociferous movement prepared to speak out in its defence. And when the New Right shifted the goal posts to require more 'non traditional ' students, credit transfer schemes, accreditation of prior learning, access courses and modularisation – the new directives were embraced with a mixture of cooperation and resignation.

A new 'enthusiasm' was generated for mature, working class, black and women students, whose educational interests and rights, ten years previously, it had seemed like a Marxist/Communist/Radical feminist heresy to promote. But also resignation because, short of taking early retirement, there seemed to be little other alternative but to go along with the new directives. Those of us who had spent many years arguing for access to the opportunities of university education for those groups of students who were conventionally excluded, and for the transformation of the culture and curriculum of university education to recognise student diversity – especially in terms of class, 'race' and gender[23] – knew that the new Access industry was more about 'jobs for the boys' and about quantity than rather than quality.[24] And that schemes concerned with credit accumulation and modularisation only made sense if you viewed education as a commodity to be collected like lottery tickets – as quickly and as mechanistically as possible – in case you should take time to think, or engage in critical analysis, or begin to make the kind of connections with others which might lead to collective action for social change.

The price paid for 'upgrading' former polytechnics to universities and spreading modularisation like wildfire has been to reduce the number of hours in which a student can expect to be taught; increase the size of groups to effectively eliminate any other teaching method except lectures; and remove all but tokenistic responsibility for student growth and emotional development, by eliminating the pastoral and personal tutor function, and splintering the possibility of a 'learning community' into a post-modernist nightmare of atomised and unrelated fragments. As 'self-directed study' methods replace human contact, and human teaching gives way to computer technology, the potential for student alienation and drop out can only increase. Despite, and some would say because of, the contradiction which is everywhere revered as 'quality control' and 'total quality management'.

As fewer and fewer teachers teach more and more people, it seems increasingly probable that output might exceed demand. In such circumstances the qualifications being gained become correspondingly irrelevant and obsolete, not to mention the notable absence of significant opportunities gained as a consequence of simply surviving the process. In such circumstances it feels possible to explain the country's obsession with the National Lottery as some kind of metaphor which appears to provide about as realistic an assessment of 'changing one's life' as any other! Meanwhile, the recognition by the rich and famous of the allegation that the University of Huddersfield, for example, can't possibly be regarded as the same as the University of Oxford, or even Warwick, has encouraged the setting up of a new super league of around twelve ancient and aspiring universities, who will pay their staff more and charge additional fees, to promote their exclusive excellence and superiority, as the market again rises to the challenge of 'flexible specialisation' as distinct from mass production.[25]

Writing in *Adults Learning* in October 1993, in response to my appeal to those who were still left' and working to offer alternatives to New Right orthodoxy in adult and continuing education, Malcolm Barry[26] praised others like himself who had 'kept their heads down' and worked 'on the inside' to make the best of what was possible. His caricature of those still operating in the radical tradition was of latter day loonies now reafflicted with political correctness, who had persuaded no one but themselves about the importance of the class struggle or women's liberation, and who had totally misjudged the mood of the working class and their obvious enthusiasm for the promises of increased affluence under the Tories.

Of course it was not simply the socialist visions of the radical tradition which got steam-rollered by the relentless rush to the right during the eighties and early nineties. The GLC and ILEA could not prevent themselves being disbanded. Trade Unions floundered as restrictive legislation stripped them of their powers and room to manoeuvre. Local Authorities were penalised for exercising local democratic mandates to contradict government directives, until they too were left in the position of administering centralised policies which many of them did not like but were powerless to prevent. Quangos replaced democratically elected and publically accountable bodies. Citizens became clients, purchasing services from an increasingly privatised 'public' sector with charters to identify their rights as consumers – though not to guarantee them. Wage councils were abolished. The social chapter wasn't signed. The welfare state was systematically restructured. Compulsory Competitive Tendering in the public sector and the introduction of new contracts in the Further Education sector all helped to reduce wages, increase working hours, deskill workers, and further discipline an already demoralised workforce. De-regulation in industry, in the guise of removing unnecessary red tape conspired, with everything else, to turn Britain into one of the lowest low wage, long hours economies in Europe. I could go on.

In the face of this kind of onslaught it is not surprising that the Great Tradition gave in and that the radical tradition in adult education did not, by itself, save the day. But what is surprising, and well worth celebrating, is that despite an extremely cold climate for the left in recent years, and despite widespread accommodation to the right by liberals in education, the radical tradition has survived. John McIlroy makes the point very well.[27] He reminds those like Barry[28] who have boasted about 'keeping their heads down' , and who have consigned the radical tradition to stereotype, that quite a lot of us are still around. We haven't 'kept our heads down' but we have continued to work against the grain in a committed way, according to principle, and with principles, in the pursuit of principles – without being excluded. The publication of *Adult Learning, Critical Intelligence and Social Change* in 1995 is in itself a testimony to the continuing presence of the radical tradition at the cutting edge of adult education theory and practice. Just as it always was. And in ways which have survived the Thatcher and Major years. Offering alternative analyses, evidence and proposals about how, in the current context, we continue to pursue the goals of radical praxis and critical intelligence, concerned to raise consciousness and provide tools for liberation in anticipation of the 'practice of freedom' which Freire talked about, and with which 'men and women can deal creatively with reality and discover how to participate in the transformation of their world'.

Notes and References

1.   Jane Thompson, Learning, Liberation and Maturity, in *Adults Learning*, (Vol 4 no 9 May 1993).
2.   Paulo Freire, *Pedagogy of the Oppressed*, (Harmondsworth, Penguin. 1972).
3.   Keith Jackson, Communities Facing Crisis – Is Adult Education Facing the Challenge?, in *Adult Education, Critical Intelligence and Social Change*, (ed) Marjorie Jane and Mayo Thompson, (NIACE, 1995).
4.   Thompson 1993 op cit.
5.   Richard Johnson, Really Useful Knowledge: Radical Education and Working Class Culture 1790–1848, in *Working Class Culture: Studies in History and Theory*, (ed) Clarke, Critcher and Johnson, (Hutchinson 1979).
6.   Poor Man's Guardian No 35 March 1832.
7.   (ed) Mayo and Thompson 1995 op cit
8.   Jackson 1995 op cit
9.   Fordham, Poulton and Randle, *Learning Networks in Adult Education: Non Formal Education on a Housing Estate*, (RKP, 1979).
10.   Jane Thompson (ed) *Adult Education for a Change*, (Hutchinson, 1980).
11.   Jane Thompson, *Learning Liberation: Women's Response to Men's Education*, (Croom Helm, 1983).
12.   Jane Thompson, *Adult Education and the Disadvantaged*, in (ed) Thompson 1980.
13.   Jennifer Rogers, *Adults Leaning*, (2nd Edition OUP 1977), and although this would not be the view expressed by him now, Michael Newman, *Poor Cousin: A Study of Adult Education*, (Allen and Unwin, 1979).

14. Nell Keddie, *Adult Education – An Ideology of Individualism*, in (ed) Thompson 1980 op cit.
15. Keith Jackson, Adult Education and Social Action, in (ed) Jones and Mayo, *Community Work One* (RKP)
16. Tom Lovett, *Adult Education, Community Development and the Working Class*, (Ward Lock 1975).
17. Geoff Brown, *Independence and Incorporation: The Labour College Movement and the Workers Education Association before the Second World War*, in (ed) Thompson 1980 op cit.
18. Poor Man's Guardian No 137 25th Sept 1834.
19. Rebecca O'Rourke, *All Equal Now?*, in (ed) Mayo and Thompson 1995 op cit.
20. For a discussion about the ways in which market forces as they have been embraced in adult education have encouraged the commodification of knowledge to the detriment of the learning process, see Keith Jackson in (ed) Mayo and Thompson 1995 op cit.
21. Taking Liberties Collective, *Learning the Hard Way – Women's Oppression in Men's Education*, (MacMillan, 1989).
22. ibid
23. Jane Thompson, The Cost and Value of Higher Education to Working Class Women, in (ed) Sylvia Harrop, *Oxford and Working Class Education*, (Nottingham University 1987)
24. Taking Liberties Collective op cit
25. Currently referred to as the Russell Group – because of their regular meeting place in the Russell Hotel, London – this group are in the process of establishing, by special advertising campaigns and recruitment strategies, a 'super group' of universities which will distinguish themselves in terms of alleged excellence and disassociate themselves from the rest.
26. Malcolm Barry, Learning, Humility and Honesty, in *Adults Learning*, (October 1993)
27. Preface (ed) Mayo and Thompson 1995 op cit
28. Barry op cit

'Really useful knowledge': linking theory and practice

(Originally published in *Radical Learning For Liberation*,
Maynooth Adult and Community Education
Occasional series 1996)

In October 1996 preparations were afoot for the World Conference on Adult
Education and Lifelong Learning to take place in Hamburg in 1997. In anticipation
of this event AONTAS, the National Committee for Development Education in
Ireland and St Patrick's College, Maynooth organised a national conference on the
theme of Empowerment and Action. Opened by President Mary Robinson and
closed by Paul Belanger, the Director of the UNESCO Institute for Education,
Thompson gave the keynote address in which she outlines the political and
educational context in which a radical learning agenda concerned with participation,
citizenship and democracy should be placed. As always she draws upon the roots of
the radical tradition in adult education, in progressive social movements concerned
with 'really useful knowledge', critical intelligence, emancipation and social change.
She argued for a renewed determination to build an agenda for lifelong learning based
on political education, in the interests of all those excluded from participation in
decision making and with decreasing control over their own lives. Her address was
subsequently published in the Maynooth Adult and Community Education Series
collection called **Radical Learning for Liberation.**

'Really useful knowledge': linking theory and practice

In the run up to the forthcoming American Presidential elections a bemused British journalist – Charles Wheeler– asks one of Bob Dole's closest advisers 'Why has it taken Bob Dole so long to get round to telling us about his principles and about the kinds of concerns he feels deeply about? We've had no sense so far of a man who is informed or guided by anything other than the immediate' (*Newsnight*, August 16 1996). The adviser replies that Dole is 'a doer' – so busy with 'the mechanics of politics' – 'the day to day demands of getting things done'. Being responsible for 'the mechanics' and 'getting things done' means you don't have a lot of time (apparently) to think very much about the greater scheme of things, why you make some choices rather than others, where your actions fit, what might be the consequences of what you do. We are meant to be impressed by 'a practical man' who rolls up his shirt sleeves and who is quick off the mark when it comes to getting things done. John Major has been quick off the mark in cultivating the same approach as he takes off his jacket, rolls up his sleeves, climbs onto his soap box and sets about answering pre-arranged questions from a carefully invited audience – most recently from the stage of the Tory party conference in Bournemouth (Bournemouth, October 1996). A strategy supposed to indicate practical politics, the common touch. 'Did you like it?' He grins enthusiastically. Desperately trying to reinforce the presentation of himself as 'Honest John – the boy from Brixton' who does what's best for Britain without getting too tied up by philosophy or ideology. Unlike Tony Blair who is still associated in many people's minds – inaccurately as it happens – with ideas that derive from socialism.

In the case of Dole the existence of any grander narrative is denied – almost as a testimony to action rather than theory. Probably it's not so surprising. Politics on both sides of the Atlantic in recent years have been characterised by short termism and pragmatism; revealing the cynicism of bland-faced re-definitions of the latest U turn, enforced resignation or scandal whilst skilfully avoiding the principled point; responding to what is immediate and leaving the medium or long term future to take care of itself. Or to someone else to sort out. Especially in relation to the environ-ment. Short term thinking in Britain currently finds the Tories embarrassingly keen to sell off and get rid of anything and everything which still remains within the public sector, before an in-coming Labour Government can get their hands on it –

including British Rail, the administration of the Social Security system, Ministry of Defence housing, and the Post Office. Whilst the Labour Party is busily shedding its philosophic commitment to historic left-of-centre principles for fear of being considered too dangerous, too visionary, too radical or too socialist by those whose votes they want to count on.

On both sides of the Atlantic the struggle for political power is being contested by individuals who seem to grow increasingly similar to each other (in terms of ethnicity, class, gender and ideas), with similar allegiances to corporate interests, and who seem more and more concerned to represent only those groups who have the same kind of stake as themselves in what is currently defined as society. Leaving the ones who are left – 'the rest' and 'the others' – more and more excluded. In the US this means that on a good day almost half the population will not exercise their vote in presidential elections and more than half won't bother to vote in congressional and senate elections. (That's if they're even registered.) Not because they are apathetic or disillusioned or stupid. But because the circumstances of their existence has little or no bearing on the agenda of either of the two presidential candidates and does not feature within the priorities of either of the two main parties which govern the United States. Why should urban ghetto dwellers, without jobs and without welfare, or Native Americans whose lands have been plundered, or Mexican immigrants who are denied citizenship rights, or rural black cotton pickers, housed in shacks along the muddy flatlands of the Mississippi, go through the motions of voting for individuals and parties which have little knowledge of their lives, and even less interest in finding out, except to keep them in check? Why would they be persuaded that their vote might 'make a difference' when they have no evidence to support the accuracy of such an obvious piece of ideology? In such circumstances, despite the platitudes and rhetoric about democracy, the widespread non-participation in voting by groups who have been effectively disenfranchised is not actually seen as a major cause for concern by those whose interests are reflected in the political system. Not voting is a consequence, and has by now become a necessary characteristic, of what counts as democracy, and which sustains the particular brand of unrepresentation established as a political system in the United States.

In Britain the trends are similar though not yet so extreme. Seventeen years of right wing Conservative governments have deepened the divisions between rich and poor; between those living in 'traditional families' and those who do not; between those who have jobs and roofs over their heads and those who do not; between those who are white and those who are black. Probably also between those who are young and male, who are educated in run-down schools lacking adequate resources, who are the ready targets for drugs and unfulfilled consumer aspirations, who have few prospects of either getting a job or buying into the housing market – and those who are female or older, living in the same neighbourhoods, whose communities are being destroyed by the pressures of poverty, unemployment, hopelessness and increasing competition for scarce resources. These are divisions which in turn cement distinctions between those who do and who don't see any purpose in getting too excited about politics. For people without much recognisable power there is no obvious connection between putting a cross on a ballot paper and changing their experience of society. In Margaret Thatcher's immortal words 'there is no such thing as society' and by definition less and less reason to assume any responsibility for anyone other than oneself. Whether one has power or not. Hers' is something of a non-society, in which minorities who live in poverty, like single parents (mostly women), the elderly (mostly women), young unemployed, people with the kind of disabilities which prevent them from working and in some cases from looking after themselves, as well as different ethnic minorities (who can be found in all the other categories as well) are termed by some 'an underclass' and by others 'scroungers'. Whatever the label, these are groups of people who have less and less reason to vote in conventional elections for politicians whose world view is increasingly shaped by the assumption that democracy is about representation rather than participation, that charters can guarantee citizens' rights, that legislation concerned with the protection of welfare provision, workers' rights, environmental sanity, and even human rights, must always, it seems, be subject to restrictions on public spending, the promotion of free market competition and the maintenance of a strong and centralised state committed to defending corporate profits.

In such circumstances politicians like Dole and Clinton in the United States do not need to articulate the theories which inform their policies. They are implicit. Their actions speak for themselves and have been understood as such by all of those who take no interest in elections. That's why they've voted with their feet. In Britain, and in other advanced industrialised societies for all I know, which are similarly committed to free market economics and restrictions on public spending, the slide towards political systems which operate on the basis of widespread non-participation, especially by those who have little stake in what is on offer, is 'a price worth paying' according to those whose social and economic advantage is secured by such arrangements. In these circumstances, minority groups of numerous kinds, with little purchase on power, and few advocates in high places, are easy enough to stereotype and to hold responsible for their own alleged deficiencies. It is commonplace, for example, according to dominant definitions of social reality, to account for the continuing inequalities between men and women, including increased levels of male violence and child sexual abuse, as being the choice of women who are 'their own worst enemies' or else the fault of nasty feminists who wear 'the wrong kind of clothes' and 'can't agree among themselves' about what should be done. It is assumed that the widespread demoralisation of entire communities by unemployment, cuts in public spending, poor health born of poverty, restrictive legislation and the intensification of punitive policing policies, is in fact the result of apathy, welfare dependency, a general decline in morality, poor parenting skills and the absence of any sense of personal responsibility. In such communities increasing numbers of people don't vote and don't readily participate in the processes of decision making which affect their lives. And whilst conventional wisdom denounces them for their fecklessness and pathological deficiencies, the gulf between those who *do* have recognisable interests to defend, and those whose material conditions are barely taken seriously, continues to widen.

Meanwhile political recourse to pragmatism, dignified as some kind of virtue which is said to 'get things done', disguises the extent to which underlying, profound *"learning"*

and quite self-conscious theoretic principles have actually determined the character of what is taking shape.

Those who are concerned about education will have noticed the same preoccupation in recent years with 'getting things done' rather than 'wasting time' on theories and debating philosophy: students into courses, throughput, output, progression routes, research profiles, accreditation schemes, calculations of competence, quality assurance, performance indicators, league tables, the appointment of management consultants, the development of marketing strategies, the measurement of everything that moves on a five point scale – all turned into statistics and graphs designed to produce efficiency savings and to release money from government funding agencies. At the same time education is being transformed into training. Judgements regarding excellence are increasingly determined on behalf of employers, and measured by inspectors employed by government-appointed quangos, who are required to stimulate competition and to establish financial targets built upon systems of penalties. Academics have become managers. Managers need have no previous 'hands-on experience' of education. Students and adult learners are spoken of as consumers. Teachers are regarded as potential revolutionaries and/or incompetents, who need to be motivated by the threat of losing their jobs, and monitored by excessive amounts of bureaucracy, as a way of using up their energy and distracting them from exercising too much critical intelligence. Like their teachers, students and learners are generally required to think as little as possible, to question even less, and to concentrate on accumulating credits and developing competencies which can be assessed by forms that can be measured by machines. As more and more people collect credits (rather like lottery tickets) which lead to qualifications that are widely considered to be totally unconnected to mind-expanding or life-transforming experiences – not to mention having little or no relationship to interesting, useful or well paid employment (if at all) – it would now seem a matter of real urgency to consider what all of this might signify. Especially if one retains some illusions about participation being a necessary ingredient of democracy. And some conviction that education can also be a weapon in the war against poverty. A weapon which might indeed be used to overcome discrimination, exploitation, exclusion and violence. Which can assist in the process of transforming societies based on inequalities, vested interests and injustice into societies in which all citizens are more directly involved in the decision making which shapes their lives. Not simply as individuals who, in the spirit of free enterprise and self-reliance, have personal responsibilities and duties to perform, and who become locked into competition for scarce resources which are frequently secured at the expense of others. But as members of collectivities which share material and social conditions that derive from the recognition of interdependence and mutual regard. And which are based on the simple conviction that no one is truly free until we all are. A conviction grounded in shared social and communal responsibilities, and the expectation of generalised participation in decision making, however local. Which is guided by a vision that extends beyond the boundaries of what *is* to what *might be* and to the kind of understandings which take account of wider, international and global considerations.

You may by now be wondering what all this has got to do with 'really useful knowledge' and 'linking theory and practice'. Social and political systems which create exclusion and lack of participation in decision making seriously damage peoples lives. People don't on the whole get angry. Creative anger could be constructive. They get demoralised or disaffected. We might like to think that communities in crisis automatically develop a wonderful 'sense of togetherness' and 'community spirit' which 'keeps them going' despite the odds. But they are just as likely – more likely perhaps – to release feelings of frustration and alienation upon each other rather than on the structural and political causes of their hopelessness. Men living in communities which are in crisis initiate more criminal activity at the expense of each other, more domestic violence, more racist attacks. Their communities are the breeding grounds for anti-democratic and extremist responses to the accumulation of grievances born of economic depression and lack of recognition. These are not the kind of responses which education can resolve. But they are the kind of circumstances in which 'particular kinds of education' might have a part to play. And by this I don't mean league tables and quality assurance mechanisms. Or aromatherapy for beginners. I mean political education.

In adult education there is a long tradition, dating back to at least the nineteenth century, even longer if we include the writing of Mary Wolstonecraft, concerned with the relationship between education and social change. The radical tradition in adult education has argued not simply for knowledge which is deemed to be 'the best that has been thought and said' – which is the basis of the extra-mural and liberal traditions. Or for knowledge that is vocational and practical – in order to make people into more skilful and responsible workers – which is the antecedent of the current pre-occupation with training. Or for knowledge which is devoid of any social context but is related to 'personhood' and 'individual self-fulfilment' – the concern of the essentially American 'human growth' school of thinking popular in the seventies. The radical tradition in adult education judges 'the usefulness' of knowledge in relation to its contribution to assisting social and political change. Especially in relation to those whose social, material and political conditions are based on oppression, inequality or exploitation. All words which are fairly unfashionable in these days of post-modern, free market and entrepreneurial thinking. But not – I think – obsolete as lived conditions. When Chartists and Christian socialists and co-operators and feminists and early trade union organisers argued for working class and women's education in the nineteenth century they wanted 'really useful knowledge' that would help them to understand both the nature of their present condition and how to get out of it. 'Really useful knowledge' was political knowledge which could be used to challenge the relations of oppression and inequality from which they suffered. In this sense arguments about the liberationary possibilities of education have a long history within the agendas of progressive political movements concerned with overcoming structural injustices and inequalities.

The radical tradition in adult education based on 'really useful knowledge' implies the development of critical thinking, the recognition of human agency, political growth and the confidence to challenge what is generally taken for granted as inevitable. It means deriving theory from the authority of lived material experience, and using it in ways which connect with the similar or related experiences of others,

↗ *social change*

in order to establish a 'critical mass' which can join together to develop collective forms of social action to achieve political change. The emphasis is not on 'competitive individualism' or the pursuit of 'individual rights' at the expense of others. But on communal responses to confronting related oppressions and to promoting change. It's about – another old fashioned word – the significance of praxis, of relating theory to practice, in which one informs the other, in a continuing and dialectical process of making changes on the basis of applying critical intelligence to what is understood from experience – in ways that re-constitute both the situation and the subject. Deriving theory from experience and in turn relating it to practice is far from being a crude mechanical or behaviourist approach. It allows for the exploration of 'meaning' and of how people 'make sense' of their lived experiences. It allows for comparisons to be made with the meanings articulated by others. It can connect the understanding of individuals and collectivities of individuals in ways that create a critical mass. It also has something useful to contribute to the understanding of what constitutes power. Power does not lie simply in the remit of dominant groups who download it – so to speak – onto less powerful victims. It does operate in this way, and structural supports for the accumulation and administration of power are clearly the backdrop against which any opportunities for the redistribution of power, the renegotiation of power-based relationships, and the recognition of available room in which to manoeuvre, must be measured.

But the exercise of power, and what might be re-defined as power, is also present within all of us, and within the relationships we make with each other. To be exercised in more or less oppressive or more or less egalitarian ways. Focused with energy and precision, and informed by the determination 'to get out from under', the power within us can be released in the service of liberation just as possibly as it can be constrained by feelings of despair or alienation.

Social changes are not simply determined by structural conditions. Or by significant individuals with superior qualities of leadership or charisma or ruthlessness. The history of social movements is a history of people operating in the cracks of superstructures. Of using the energies generated at the margins of systems and organisations. Of exercising considerable imagination, critical thinking, subversion and undutiful behaviour to de-stabilise and de-construct the authority of the inevitable. All of them ways of 'taking back control' based on the inter-relationship between consciousness and courage, between theory and practice. Taking back control and joining with others in collective action to achieve change is at the root of concepts like participation and democracy. It finds its impetus in human agency and can transform people's lives. As well as transforming views about oneself.

All of which might sound enormously idealistic and highly abstract. But anyone who has experienced what it feels like to say 'No' to different forms of oppression, or to engage creatively and seriously with others in a piece of social action concerned to get something established or something changed which more powerful interests have determined must continue, will know how contagious the release of human possibility can be. Even in defeat there is the further possibility of making progress, so long as the expectation of having collective rights to participation and exercising some control over one's material conditions are allowed to enter the collective conscious-ness. This is precisely what Freire has discussed as conscientisation in relation to education as the practice of freedom (Freire, 1972). It's what bell hooks refers to as 'transgression' in which the academy, the classroom, the neighbourhood drop-in centre – anywhere in which learning is taking place – may not be paradise, but is ' a place where paradise can be created . . . With all its limitations (the classroom/the neighbourhood/the drop in centre) remains a location of possibility (where we can) collectively go beyond boundaries, to transgress'. According to bell hooks this is also 'education as the practice of freedom' (hooks 1994 p207).

And just in case you imagine that the pursuit of social change from below, based on conscientisation, the development of critical intelligence and the courage to be undutiful in the interests of transgression, all implies a form of 'really useful knowledge' which is only related to the disciplines of politics, economics and social science, I would remind you of what the late great Audre Lorde had to say about making new knowledge and about developing our own ways of doing things. Even she might have stopped short at the prospect of 'aromatherapy for beginners' being regarded as having any political or emancipatory significance but she would have encouraged us to make use of every available opportunity to connect popular educa-tion to the self-conscious struggle for popular liberation from oppressions. She was not talking simply about access and required us to remember 'that the master's tools will never dismantle the master's house' (Lorde, ed Moraga and Anzaldua, 1981 p98). In other words, that access to wider power, without some transformation of the systems of power, will not be sufficient to deliver the kinds of changes we might envision. Thinking beyond conventional forms of wisdom and the alleged logic of present systems is a further variation on the theme of 'really useful knowledge' and is con-nected to what another black poet, June Jordan, has to say in relation to the importance of poetry, political consciousness and language. She says, 'good poetry and successful revolutions change our lives. (But) you cannot compose a good poem or wage a revolution without changing consciousness. And you cannot alter consciousness unless you attack the language that you share with your enemies and invent a language that you share with your allies'. (Jordan, 1994 pp70–1)

Part of the residual problem with liberal as distinct from radical approaches to the dilemmas posed by education for social change is the widespread assumption that what you need to do is 'modify your language' (and your appearance and your dress code) to lull potential power holders into a false sense of security about your reasonableness and moderation. Even to change your language, so that it is less 'confrontational' ie, less associated with 'unpopular' world views like feminism, social-ism or Marxism. The problem with calling women's rights 'gender studies', or lesbian-ism 'sexual preference', or anti-discrimination 'equal opportunities', or unemployment 'flexibility', or redundancy 'efficiency savings', or privatisation 'consumer choice', or education 'training', or democratic rights 'customer contracts' or 'client's charters', however, is that the modification of the language changes its meaning and its impact. It also means that you quickly forget the point at which you began to adopt the language of the enemy as a strategy to gain acceptance, with the intention of 'work-ing from within'. It soon becomes 'second nature' to you, and the repertoire with which you then make sense of the world. Except that you are likely to be making sense of the world in a significantly altered way, as you become progressively wedded to the concepts and concerns of those whose interests might be very different to your own, and into which you have now become incorporated. 'Really useful knowledge' in this sense implies vigilance, imagination, courage and taking trouble to be free.

The ideas related to the notion of 'really useful knowledge' also offers us a way of thinking about adult education now, as a form of popular education for democracy, and in relation to debates about active citizenship and more widespread participation in decision making. Debates which might have relevance at a local level – to inform social action campaigns; in political movements of various kinds; as antidotes to the widespread domination of public life by white, middle class, able-bodied men – but also to address the responsibilities implied in the protection of human rights, environmentalism and globalisation. In this sense I would recommend you to take a look at the report recently produced by the Women and Citizenship Research Group in association with the Equal Opportunities Commission for Northern Ireland called *Women and Citizenship: Power, Participation and Choice* (EOC, 1995).

The research starts with the reluctance of women to say they engage in politics, or at least Politics with a capital P – a reluctance which is widespread across Europe. Reluctance should not be read as ignorance or apathy, however. It partly stems from constitutional arrangements and partly from historic (and patriarchal) mechanisms of exclusion. It partly implies a definition of what constitutes politics and which doesn't take account of, for example, community activism, campaigning, membership of voluntary organisations and pressure groups or social movements. It also stems from the ways in which power is mediated within communities by additional considerations of gender, age, ethnicity and the like. Frequently women have been required to subsume their interests as women to other loyalties which might be defined by others as 'more important'.

Citizenship is, by the way, one of those buzz words which can mean very different things to different people and needs to be used with caution. The Tory government in Britain uses citizenship to preach ideologies of self-help and self-reliance and is intended to promote personal contributions to the common good. According to modern Conservatism, citizens' rights are seen as being analogous to consumers' rights, in ways that can be underwritten by public charters. Except that patients' charters have done very little to guarantee an effective health system which responds quickly and appropriately when people are sick. Travellers' charters don't make the trains run on time, or increase safety standards undermined by de-regulation, or address the imminent collapse of the transport infrastructure. Consumers' charters haven't prevented fat cats from making enormous profits out of privatising public utilities or persuaded *them* to make personal contributions to the common good. Individualised complaints procedures, administered by quangos, don't compensate for taking power away from democratically-elected local authorities or restricting trade union activities. Definitions of citizenship which require people to behave themselves and do what the state wants are not good reasons in themselves for promoting active citizenship.

The same problems emerge in adopting an uncritical enthusiasm for an 'individual rights' mentality. In Britain the pressure group Liberty (once the National Council for Civil Liberties) retains an essentially liberal and libertarian attitude to protecting people's rights, and is based on a philosophy – liberalism – which has got a lot more in common with Thatcherism than many people would like to imagine. Personally I cannot accept that an individual's right to participate in the production and dissemination of child pornography, for example, can simply be viewed as a matter of personal conscience or choice. Or that it's unfair to arrest sex tourists in Britain on the basis of what they get up to in the Philippines and Thailand. Discussions about rights which are expressed only in individual terms, or in relation to the concerns of specific groups, don't get us very far along the road when it comes to challenging structural oppressions like racism, imperialism and sexism.

The concerns of the Women and Citizenship research project are somewhat more modest. But extremely important. The main focus of the research is about the long exclusion of women from the sphere of legal and political rights, and from active participation in decision making bodies in the public sphere. A secondary focus deals with what might be the significance of women's greater inclusion. The report notes the absence of women in public life in Northern Ireland compared to men, and compared to the situation in Great Britain, which is in itself not very inspiring. The writers also consider the Republic of Ireland in which some changes for the better have occurred during the last twenty years. Most notably the election of Mary Robinson as President and increasing numbers of women in the Dail – 12% in 1994 as against 7.8% in 1989. (As in Britain – still some way to go, I would say.) In discussing some of these concerns with women's groups of various kinds the report is able to make a number of recommendations which would give women more influence and more representation. These involve recommendations directed towards women's organisations, towards political parties and politicians, and towards policy makers in the voluntary and statutory sectors. It is interesting to note the extent to which the recommendations deal with issues about power. And so far as the contribution made by education is concerned, how important it is seen to be to develop content that is related to raising political, economic and feminist awareness, as well as developing the kinds of skills which can turn heightened awareness into effective practice. The main education recommendation, in fact, is to promote political education, based on what I would call 'really useful knowledge', with a view to increasing the direct participation of women in decision making and public life. In practice this would mean transforming the culture of existing political institutions and decision making bodies – not simply to make them more women-friendly and reflective of women's issues, but in order to reconstitute some of the assumptions about what counts as political concerns – from a women's point of view. This would provoke many more debates – and in turn policies – about environmental issues, community concerns, child care, women's employment rights, reproductive and health rights, and issues concerning violence against women, for example, than is currently on the agendas of most malestream political parties. People in the audience will have their own ideas about what else a more gender-balanced agenda might include.

This then is just one example. The work packs currently being produced by the Popular Education for Democracy Project at the Department of Continuing

Education in Leeds is another. Neither is a blueprint. Different circumstances and different cultural contexts require different responses no doubt. Except the underlying principle remains the same. As adult educators, community development workers, volunteers and community activists we are all cultural workers whose energies and services can be called upon, as particular kinds of resources, to be used in the interests (or as inhibitors) of political change. We are likely to have no greater insight into what might constitute emancipatory learning than people whose communities, and whose life very often depends upon it. Certainly our role is not to direct or control the energies which are released – although we might want to lend solidarity and recognise commonalities where appropriate. Or express dissent. Certainly we all have significant oppressions of our own to be dealing with before we start thinking we can tell others what to do. But we ought to know about creating the kinds of learning spaces, and providing the kinds of content and learning opportunities, which enable groups of people facing oppressions and discrimination to identify what would be 'really useful knowledge' for them, in order to better understand their situations and to take action in pursuit of change. To turn theory into practice. As all of us in this room must also do.

Disclaiming theory in the pursuit of practicalities and 'rolling up the sleeves' to 'get things done' is a form of action without reflection. It sustains systems of oppression rather than acknowledging the complexities of how power and ideologies operate. It doesn't, in the end, do anyone we care about any favours. It's also bad faith.

Which brings me back to the point with which I began. Just because Bob Dole and Tony Blair and John Major are playing coy about the theories which inform their actions, it doesn't mean to say they haven't got any. They would be more honest – and in the end, be held in higher regard by those they want to persuade, if they took the trouble to acknowledge them.

Notes and References

1. Paulo Freire, *Pedagogy of the Oppressed*, (Harmondsworth Penguin 1972).
2. bell hooks, *Teaching to Transgress : Education and the Practice of Freedom*, (Routledge 1994).
3. June Jordan, Who's Rocking the Boat?, *Ms Magazine* (March-April 1994).
4. Audre Lorde, in (ed) Moraga and Anzaldua, *This Bridge Called my Back: Writings by Radical Women of Color*, (Persephone Press 1981).
5. Popular Education for Democracy Project, Dept of Continuing Education, University of Leeds.
6. Women and Citizenship Research Group, *Women and Citizenship: Power, Participation and Choice*. (Equal Opportunities Commission for Northern Ireland 1995).

Also published by NIACE:

Adults count too: Mathematics for empowerment
Roseanne Benn
ISBN 1 86201 007 2
Publication date: June 1997, approx 176pp, £14.95

More and more adults are learning mathematics, either for work-related purposes, or as a qualification leading to a desired course of study. *Adults count too* examines the low level of numeracy in our society, the reasons why this is critical and the forces acting on adults which contribute to this state of affairs. Written to encourage the development of a curriculum which is tailored to the priorities and lives of individuals, Benn argues that mathematics is not a value-free construct, but is imbued with elitist notions which exclude and mystify. The book seeks alternative approaches to teaching mathematics which recognise the sophisticated mathematical techniques and ideas used in everyday work, domestic and leisure.

This book will be of interest to adult educators who teach mathematics or to mathematics educators who teach adults.

Imagining tomorrow: Adult education for transformation
Marjorie Mayo
ISBN 1 86201 006 4
Publication date: June 1997, 184pp, £14.95

A study of the increasing importance of community and workplace adult education in the First and Third worlds. Mayo looks at the impact of globalisation, economic restructuring and the enhanced role of community and voluntary organisations in the provision of education. She presents the case for wider understanding of the context and possibilities for local development as part of longer-term strategies for transformation.

Mayo looks at the implications of adult learning for sustainable development for social justice, defined by local communities themselves. She takes case studies from Tanzania, Cuba, India and Nicaragua as well as from the industrialised 'North' to illustrate her themes. The book concludes by focussing on issues of culture, identity, diversity and changing consciousness; and the role of community education in strengthening collective confidence to effect social transformation.

Ethics and education for adults in a late modern society
Peter Jarvis
ISBN 1 86201 014 5 (hbk)
ISBN 1 86201 015 3 (pbk)
Publication date: June 1997, 192pp, £35.00 (hbk), £17.95 (pbk)

Peter Jarvis analyses recent developments in the education of adults from an ethical perspective. Based upon the argument that there is only one universal good, and that all other moral goods are cultural and relative, he develops the position that education for adults is a site within which human morality is worked out. Examining both traditional topics, such as teaching and learning, and more recent ones, such as the education market, distance education and the learning society, Jarvis argues that educators need to be critically aware of the ethical implications of these developments. This is a topical book which should be of interest to everybody involved in education at every level and every age group.

Peter Jarvis is currently Professor of Continuing Education at the University of Surrey and Adjunct Professor of Adult Education at the University of Georgia, USA. He was previously Head of Department of Educational Studies at the University of Surrey. He is the author and editor of more than twenty books. He is also the editor of *The International Journal of Lifelong Education*.

Electronic pathways: Adult learning and the new communication technologies
Edited by Jane Field
ISBN 186201 008 0
1997, 176pp, £14.95

What does the information society really mean for adult learning? A rapidly-growing range of communications technologies is being developed to support the adult learner. Telematics applications can have an impact on education, leisure and work, but adult educators and others involved in working with adult learners need practical help if they are to make the most of the opportunities.

This is the first book to place the new information and communications technologies firmly in the context of adult learning. It is written by adult educators who have used the new technologies to widen access to learning and promote independent learning. They have seen that it is possible to offer different ways to communicate and support learning, whether in college, the home, the workplace or other settings.

Case studies provide examples of the pitfalls involved, good practice identified and the opportunities available. The book is an accessible, informative and practical resource for all who are professionally concerned with developing adult learning.

A full publications catalogue is available from NIACE at 21 De Montfort Street, Leicester, LE1 7GE, England. Alternatively visit our Web site on the Internet: **http://www.niace.org.uk**